TOO GOOD
TO GET HIRED

TOO GOOD
TO GET HIRED

Niche Press
Indianapolis, IN

TOO GOOD TO GET HIRED: GO FROM OVERQUALIFIED TO A PERFECT FIT
Copyright © 2026 by Isaiah Hankel

All rights reserved. No part of this book may be used or reproduced in any manner whatsoever without prior written consent of the author, except as provided by the United States of America copyright law.

The author and publisher have made every effort to ensure the accuracy and integrity of the information in this book. However, neither assumes responsibility or liability for any errors, omissions, or outcomes resulting from its use. The material is provided "as is," without warranties of any kind, express or implied, including any guarantee of employment, career success, or specific results.

This book is intended solely for informational and educational purposes. It is not a substitute for professional, legal, financial, or career advice. Readers should seek qualified guidance for their individual circumstances. The author's academic or professional credentials do not create a client-professional relationship with readers.

Portions of this work may have been informed by research or drafting assistance using artificial intelligence tools. All content was reviewed and edited by the author; however, no guarantee is made as to its completeness, originality, or accuracy. The author and publisher disclaim all liability for any errors, omissions, or consequences arising from use of this information.

By reading this book, you agree to use the information at your own discretion and hold harmless the author and publisher from any claims or damages arising from its use.

For permission to reprint portions of this content or for bulk purchases, contact support@overqualified.com

Published by Niche Press; NichePress.com
Indianapolis, IN

ISBN
Hardback: 978-1-970329-03-2
Paperback: 978-1-970329-04-9
eBook: 978-1-970329-02-5

Library of Congress Cataloging-in-Publication Data on File at lccn.loc.gov

The views expressed herein are solely those of the author and do not necessarily reflect the views of the publisher.

*This book is dedicated to my family:
Laura, Zara, Eve, and Atlas.*

It's also dedicated to you and those who need you to keep going until you get your one "yes," and get into the right job for you.

CONTENTS

Preface: Careers Are More Than Paychecks · · · · · · · · · · · · · · · · · ix
Introduction: What Is the Overqualified Crisis? · · · · · · · · · · · · · · · · 1

SECTION ONE: TO THEM, YOU'RE TOO GOOD TO HIRE   5

1. Why the Hiring System Thinks You're a Problem · · · · · · · · · · 7
2. You Can't Hide from the Overqualified Problem · · · · · · · · · 13
3. Start Overcoming the Overqualified Problem
   with High Commitment · 19
4. Align Yourself with the Company's Values and Culture · · · 25
5. This Role Is Your Top Choice, Not Just One of Many · · · · · 31
6. Stop Proving Yourself Out of a Job · 37
7. Lead with Potential, Anchor with Results · · · · · · · · · · · · · · · 47
8. Learn to Be Agreeable · 53
9. Six Agreeable Statements to Get You Hired · · · · · · · · · · · · · · 61
10. There Is No Perfect Job, But There Is the Right
    One for You · 67
11. Stop Searching Job Boards, Start Following Companies · · · 73

SECTION TWO: SET A TARGET AND POSITION YOURSELF AS THE SAFE CANDIDATE   77

12. Choose Sectors First, Not Job Titles · 79
13. The Half-Page Handshake: Writing a Cover Letter
    That Gets Read · 85
14. Say Why or Say Goodbye: Overcoming Objections in
    Your Cover Letter · 91
15. A Line of Accountability: Add Two Names to Your
    Cover Letter · 95
16. The Two Real Resume Formats That Matter Today · · · · · · · 99
17. The Hybrid Resume: The New Standard for
    Overqualified Job Seekers · 105
18. The Six-Part Resume Structure Employers Love · · · · · · · · · 113
19. Think Like AI: Keyword Density and The Visual Center · 119
20. Make the Most of Your Honors, Hobbies, and
    Awards Section · 125

SECTION THREE: YOU'RE BEING PROFILED AND SCORED BY EMPLOYERS — 129

21 Your Resume and LinkedIn Profile Are
Personality Tests · 131
22 The Digital Inquisition · 137
23 How to Find and Understand Your Reputation Score · · · · · 141
24 Comments Are the New Cover Letter · · · · · · · · · · · · · · · · · · 151
25 The Hidden Power of Weak Ties and Workplace Alumni · 155
26 Say Something About *Them* First · 159
27 From Stranger to Referral: The Four Levels of
Professional Intimacy · 163

SECTION FOUR: FROM GETTING INTERVIEWS TO PASSING INTERVIEWS — 169

28 Culture Fit Is the Only Interview Assessment · · · · · · · · · · · · 171
29 Can You Sit at Every Table? · 177
30 Why You? Why Us? The Two Questions That Decide
Everything · 181
31 The Values Test · 189
32 Work Samples and Assessments · 195
33 If Your Wi-Fi Drops, So Do You: Mastering
Tech to Get Hired · 199
34 Leverage Interviews to Close the Deal · · · · · · · · · · · · · · · · · 205
35 How to Win the Salary Negotiation · · · · · · · · · · · · · · · · · · · 211
36 It Only Takes One Yes to Change Everything · · · · · · · · · · · 217
37 Start Making the 2mm Shifts That Get You Hired · · · · · · · 223

Endnotes · 227
Thank You · 231
About Isaiah Hankel · 233

PREFACE

CAREERS ARE MORE THAN PAYCHECKS

Daniel spent his career climbing the ranks of management until, one day, the credentials and experience that once opened doors started slamming them shut. Elaine led teams and built programs from the ground up, only to be told she was "not the right fit" again and again after being laid off.

Daniel and Elaine are just two of the more than 20,000 highly qualified people in their forties, fifties, and sixties I've worked with and helped get hired again after being boxed out of the job market for being "too good." After years of rejection letters, silent application portals, and interviews that ended in a handshake and nothing else, Daniel and Elaine knew they needed help. They thought the problem was them. It wasn't.

I know that because I watched this problem unfold in my own family long before I became a career consultant. When I was a kid, my parents hit the same wall that disrupted Daniel and Elaine's careers. They had stable jobs, long careers, and experience that should have secured their future. But once they reached a certain age, the market turned its back. I didn't know it at the time, but I was living through a lesson in how unforgiving the hiring system can be when it decides you're "too much."

My parents' career collapse wasn't instant. First, there were longer gaps between interviews. Then came the awkward rejections, the underpaid contract work, and the part-time jobs that barely covered the bills. My parents fought to keep us afloat, but the math never worked out. Eventually, we lost our home. My mom and sister moved in with my aunt, and my dad, my brother, and I ended up in a one-bedroom apartment across town. Some nights we ate dinner at shelters. At Christmas, the presents came from donation bins. We stood in line for government-issued cheese packed in cardboard boxes and paid for groceries with paper food stamps that looked like play money.

One morning, I woke up to the sound of our car starting outside. I thought it was being stolen. At school, I told everyone a thief had taken it. That night, my parents sat me down and told me the truth: it had been repossessed.

That moment burned itself into my memory. It wasn't just the loss of the car that stuck with me. I knew we'd lost control over our lives, and no matter how hard my parents worked, the job market had the final say.

That's when I realized something most people never have to learn so young: everything — healthcare, stability, dignity, opportunities for your kids — rests on your ability to stay competitive in the job market. Careers aren't just about paychecks. They're about survival.

I never forgot what it felt like to have our family torn apart by something so basic as not being able to find work. And when I grew up, I committed myself to making sure others wouldn't have to face the same collapse without someone in their corner.

Over the last fifteen years, I've worked with more than 20,000 people the market labeled as "overqualified." People with long executive track records, advanced degrees, or simply too many birthdays behind them. People just like Daniel and Elaine. And what I've learned is that they're not failing because they're not good enough, they're failing because they're *too good*.

The chapters that follow mirror the journey I guided Daniel and Elaine through as they worked to rejoin the workforce.

They begin where most of my clients begin: trapped in confusion and frustration, unsure why their resumes get ignored or their interviews fizzle out. Each act introduces a core truth about the hiring system; truths I've spent years discovering and refining into strategies that work.

You'll learn how overqualified candidates unintentionally prove themselves out of jobs by oversharing results, drowning hiring managers in proof, or projecting too much authority too soon. You'll discover how likability and agreeableness often matter more than raw credentials, and how simple statements can disarm the very doubts that keep you from getting hired. And you'll learn how resumes, cover letters, and even your digital footprint are read not as records, but as personality tests — signals of whether you'll fit in, whether you'll stay, and whether you'll be safe to hire.

Along the way, you'll watch Daniel and Elaine learn to shift. They discover how to lead with potential and anchor with results. How to write cover letters that sound human instead of historical. How to adapt their resumes to modern filters powered by artificial intelligence. How to network using weak ties and professional intimacy instead of spamming job boards. How to show culture fit in an interview. How to treat every interaction not as a transaction but as an audition. And how to negotiate from a place of options rather than desperation.

Woven through their stories, you'll also see mine, because the lessons I teach are not abstract. They were carved into me during the years my family struggled to hold itself together. They were sharpened over fifteen years of coaching people whose lives, marriages, and health were on the line because they couldn't get past the label of "overqualified." And they're delivered to you now in the same way I gave them to Daniel and Elaine: one act at a time, practical and personal, until the job market no longer looks like a wall but a door.

This is not a book of theory. It's a story of survival, resilience, and transformation. Each act is a chapter in Daniel and

Elaine's journey, but it's also a mirror for yours. By the end, you'll see how two people who thought they were finished, found their way back into meaningful work, not by diminishing who they were, but by repositioning themselves in ways the market could finally understand.

And that's the point I want you to carry with you as you read: your story isn't over. If you've been rejected, ignored, or dismissed, it doesn't mean you're done. It just means you need a new approach.

It only takes one yes to change everything. And as you'll see in the chapters that follow, that yes is still out there — for Daniel, for Elaine, and for you.

INTRODUCTION

WHAT IS THE OVERQUALIFIED CRISIS?

The term "overqualified" is one of the most common rejection labels in today's job market — and one of the least understood. On the surface, it sounds like a compliment that means you're too good for the job. Too experienced. Too accomplished. But the reality is far less flattering. Being called overqualified is not a reflection of your value; it's an excuse. It's a euphemism. A subtle but effective way of saying: you're not wanted here.

This rejection disproportionately affects individuals over the age of forty and especially those over fifty or sixty with substantial experience, and often with advanced degrees, in salaried, professional roles. These are candidates who, on paper, should be at the top of every recruiter's list. They've done the work, earned the credentials, built the portfolios. And yet, they're being left behind. They're not getting callbacks. They're being

> **Being called overqualified is not a reflection of your value; it's an excuse. It's a euphemism. A subtle but effective way of saying: you're not wanted here.**

ghosted after interviews. They're told, in coded language, that they're not a good fit, even when their background aligns perfectly with the role.

This phenomenon isn't just anecdotal. It's widespread. It's structural. It's systemic. And it's growing worse with each economic contraction, each wave of automation, and each generation of younger, less expensive labor entering the workforce. The Overqualified Crisis is what happens when a society decides that expertise is no longer an advantage, but a risk. That experience is something to avoid, rather than seek out. That education, if it reaches a certain level, becomes a liability.

People who have built entire careers in good faith by working hard, gaining knowledge, and increasing their capabilities are now being punished for doing exactly what society told them to do. They're being filtered out by algorithms that rank resumes based on cost-efficiency instead of competence. They're being dismissed by hiring managers who worry about retention metrics, culture fit, and perceived salary demands. And they're being marginalized by a growing belief that youth and flexibility matter more than wisdom and depth.

Many of the candidates affected by this crisis find themselves trapped in a painful paradox. They are overqualified for the roles they apply to, but in reality, they are underemployed or unemployed. They hear conflicting advice: aim lower to get in the door, but not too low or you'll appear desperate; highlight your achievements, but not so much that you seem intimidating; show enthusiasm, but not so much that it feels forced. The result is often paralysis. Candidates become stuck in a cycle of self-editing, constantly second-guessing how to present themselves to avoid being filtered out again.

It's important to understand that being labeled as overqualified rarely stems from an objective assessment of skills. Instead, it reflects a series of assumptions, most of them unspoken. Employers may assume that overqualified candidates will demand higher salaries, push back on decisions, leave as soon as a better opportunity arises, or challenge younger leaders. These concerns are often more emotional than rational, rooted in fear, insecurity, and a desire to preserve the status quo. In some cases, the label is used to avoid confronting deeper forms of bias against age, against education, or against those who don't fit neatly into a company's hierarchy.

The danger of this crisis is that it not only damages individual careers but also erodes the overall quality of the workforce. When companies systematically exclude their most experienced and educated applicants, they lower the average level of insight, judgment, and long-term thinking inside their organizations. They prioritize short-term adaptability over sustained excellence. They trade competence for compliance.

And it's not just companies that suffer. Society as a whole loses out when high-capability professionals are sidelined. Innovation slows. Institutional knowledge disappears. Younger workers are left without mentors. And the cultural narrative starts to shift from one that values hard-earned expertise to one that celebrates convenience, speed, and minimal resistance.

It's no wonder that so many overqualified candidates are choosing to leave traditional employment altogether. Many are pushed into contract work, consulting, or entrepreneurship, not because they want to be their own boss, but because it's the only option left. These paths can be rewarding, but they also come with instability, lack of benefits, and the constant need to self-market and self-fund. In effect, the system is pushing its most capable members to the margins, where their skills are less visible, less valued, and often underutilized.

Still, it's important to recognize that the Overqualified Crisis, while real, is not immutable. Being labeled as overqualified doesn't mean you're finished. It means you need to change the way you're presenting your value. You need to reframe the narrative that others are writing about you before they write you off. You need to understand the assumptions employers are making and address them head-on. And you need to learn how to translate your strengths into language that employers can hear and trust.

This book is not about hiding who you are. It's not about downplaying your accomplishments or pretending to be less than you are. It's about strategy. It's about learning how to reposition your expertise in a way that's relevant, relatable, and irresistible to hiring decision-makers. It's about speaking the language of today's job market, without compromising the depth of your knowledge or the integrity of your experience.

The Overqualified Crisis is a rejection of complexity in favor of convenience. It's a rejection of long-term investment in favor of short-term utility. And if you're one of the people caught in its grip, you need to know that your value is not diminished just because it's not being recognized. Your value is still real. It just needs to be communicated differently.

In the chapters ahead, we'll explore the unspoken fears behind the overqualified label, the ways you can reframe your approach to hiring, and the specific steps you can take to get past the bias and get back into a full-time, salaried role that reflects what you've earned and who you are.

The crisis isn't about you being overqualified. It's about a hiring system that's underprepared to understand what you bring.

SECTION ONE

TO THEM, YOU'RE TOO GOOD TO HIRE

CHAPTER 1

WHY THE HIRING SYSTEM THINKS YOU'RE A PROBLEM

I met Daniel and Elaine in a quiet corner of a coffee shop on a rainy Tuesday morning. They'd never met, but when they shook hands, I saw the same weight in their eyes. Daniel wore a suit that was too formal for a casual meeting, like he was clinging to professionalism as a shield. Elaine's bag was full of resumes printed on heavy paper — the kind you bring to an interview, not a coffee shop.

As we settled into a booth next to a window, I felt the familiar desire to help them building in my gut. I'd been helping highly qualified professionals in their forties, fifties, and sixties for more than fifteen years, and every new client meeting still felt like a fresh opportunity to give someone an opportunity to regain their livelihood — a mission I'd dedicated my life to since my parents had been shut out of the job market.

Daniel spoke first. "Sixty-seven applications in four months. Three interviews. Every time, I'm told I'm not the right fit. But my resume is bulletproof. I've led multimillion-dollar teams. I've got twenty years of results. I should be the obvious choice."

Elaine nodded. "Same here. I've targeted my resume; rewritten it a dozen times. No change. I think..." she hesitated. "I think they're afraid of me."

They weren't imagining it. Not the fear, not the rejection.

"You're not invisible," I said. "The system sees you, it just doesn't know what to do with you. And if you don't understand how the system really works, it will keep shutting you out."

THE OVERQUALIFIED CRISIS CAPTURED IN HARD DATA

It's a cruel paradox: the more qualified you are, the harder it is to get hired. That isn't a metaphor. It's not a guess. It's a documented, scientific reality. A recent study published in the *Journal of Personality and Social Psychology* found that when job candidates were perceived as "high-capability," highly experienced, highly credentialed, or simply more advanced than what a role required, they were *less likely* to be hired than lower-capability applicants, even when all other factors were equal.[1]

The researchers behind this study discovered something most hiring managers would never admit: candidates who appear "too good" for a job are viewed with suspicion. Not because of any specific flaw, but because of what they *might* do.

They might leave too soon. They might expect too much. They might act superior. They might disrupt the hierarchy. They might decline the offer, accept a competing offer, or simply get bored and walk away.

And so, employers take the path of least resistance. They pass on the most capable candidates, not because they doubt their skills, but because they fear their motives.

> **Employers take the path of least resistance. They pass on the most capable candidates, not because they doubt their skills, but because they fear their motives.**

If you've been in the job market for a while and you have a long resume, seniority, and lots of education behind you, you've felt this firsthand. You've applied to roles that match your background perfectly and heard nothing. You've aced interviews only to be told the company went with someone else. You've trimmed down your resume, reworded your title, avoided mentioning your masters degree or doctorate, and still hit a wall.

It's not in your head. The system is flagging you as a problem.

Fortunately, this bias *can* be overcome. The same study showed that high-capability candidates *can* get hired if they know how to rewrite the story that employers are telling themselves. The researchers found that when highly capable applicants took three specific actions, the hiring bias against them disappeared. Not reduced, *eliminated*. They became *more* likely to be hired than their less-qualified counterparts. Those actions are:

1. Demonstrating a high commitment to the specific role and company.
2. Aligning with the company's culture and values.
3. Showing that this role is your top choice, not your only option.

DEMONSTRATE HIGH COMMITMENT TO THE SPECIFIC ROLE AND COMPANY

Most overqualified candidates don't realize that they come across as lukewarm, too polished, too practiced, or too neutral. They talk about what they can do, but not what they *want* to do. They list their achievements, but not their enthusiasm. And so, the hiring manager wonders, *Is this job just a placeholder for them?*

To counter this, you need to go all in. Make it clear that you want *this job*, at *this company*, for *specific reasons*. Not as a steppingstone. Not as a fallback. Not as a good match for your skill set. But because it aligns with who you are, what you believe, and where you want to grow. High commitment isn't implied. It must be shown. Repeatedly. If a company is going to take a chance on someone they think is overqualified, they need to know you're not going to treat the job like a compromise.

ALIGN YOURSELF WITH THE COMPANY'S VALUES AND CULTURE

In the study, candidates who focused on how they could contribute to *organizational* success, those who expressed alignment with company culture and team dynamics, were rated much more favorably than those who emphasized individual goals or achievements. In other words, you need to show that you're not just bringing skills, you're contributing to the company's culture.

That means going beyond typical industry research when you're crafting your resume. It means using their language in your interviews. It means referencing the company's mission and connecting it to your own values. It means talking about how you collaborate, how you follow leadership, how you support teams. You can't afford to look like an outsider trying to reshape the organization from the top down. You have to present yourself as someone who understands the environment and wants to strengthen it, not overhaul it.

DEMONSTRATE THAT THIS ROLE IS YOUR TOP CHOICE, NOT YOUR ONLY OPTION

One of the biggest fears hiring managers have about high-capability candidates is that they're secretly holding out for something better. And to be fair, many are. They apply broadly. They keep doors open. They mention that they're entertaining other opportunities during interviews. And that's exactly what sinks them. Like their search for the right culture fit, employers these days aren't just hiring skill, they're hiring commitment. If they believe you'll accept another offer or back out after an offer is extended, they won't take the risk. Period.

You need to shut that door for them. Not by lying, but by clearly communicating that this role is your focus, your priority, your number one choice. Talk about how you've evaluated the market. Talk about how this company aligns with what you're looking for. Talk about the future you see for yourself in the role. Take away the uncertainty. If they don't have to wonder where you stand, they're far more likely to move forward.

This may sound frustrating. You might be thinking, *Why should I have to perform this extra emotional labor just to get a job I'm clearly qualified for?* And you're right to feel that way. You *shouldn't* have to do it. But the alternative means being misunderstood, misjudged, and left out.

The fact of the matter is that the current hiring systems are built to minimize perceived risk. And right now, you *look* risky — not because of what you've done, but because of what they assume you'll do next. If you want to change that, you have to make new assumptions easier to believe.

This isn't about playing small. It's about showing commitment, not ambivalence. Collaboration, not superiority. Focus, not distraction. It's about owning your experience *and* your intentions, at the same time.

You are not a problem. You are a solution wrapped in a misunderstood story. The data proves that when high-capability candidates shift how they show up, when they clarify their loyalty, signal alignment, and commit to the opportunity in front of them, they stop being seen as a flight risk and start being seen as the best person for the job.

The next chapters will show you how to apply these principles to every part of your job search, from your resume to your interviews to your LinkedIn profile. The hiring system doesn't fear your talent. It fears your exit.

> **The hiring system doesn't fear your talent. It fears your exit.**

CHAPTER 2

YOU CAN'T HIDE FROM THE OVERQUALIFIED PROBLEM

For a while, Elaine and Daniel talked about finding the "right fit" and waiting for "the right opportunity." But by the time we started our work together, those words had vanished. They'd both reached the point in their job search where preference gives way to survival.

Elaine confessed she'd started calculating how many more mortgage payments she could make before she'd have to sell her house. Daniel admitted he'd stopped answering calls from old colleagues because he couldn't bear to explain that he was still out of work. Both were living in the quiet panic that settles in when savings start to disappear, and confidence erodes faster than the balance in your checking account.

One night, Elaine sent me an email after midnight that said, "I've been looking at my options. I started applying to jobs at grocery stores and even the local hospital cafeteria. They're full-time."

I called her the next morning. "You could try for those jobs," I said. "But applying to lower-level jobs just makes the overqualification problem worse. And how long will you be able to work in one of those roles? How long will it be before you resent every minute of it?"

She was silent.

"You've spent twenty-five years building skills that don't belong behind a grocery store checkout station or food counter," I said.

Daniel wasn't sleeping either. He'd driven for rideshare apps for a few weeks to make ends meet, but the hours were brutal, and the pay was humiliating. "I thought I'd just do it temporarily," he told me. "But it's like quicksand. Once you start saying yes to survival jobs, you start believing that's all you can get."

Sitting in that coffee shop booth, I told them both what I tell everyone at this stage of their job search: "You cannot afford to sit this out. You can't just rely on temporary work and wait for the market to come around. You have to fight your way back into a salaried role now, before it's too late."

Elaine looked at me across the table, her voice barely above a whisper. "You really think I still can?"

"I don't think," I said. "I know. But you can't avoid the hard work of changing your approach. And you have to make the changes now."

YOU CAN'T ESCAPE OR DELAY YOUR NEED FOR A HIGH-QUALITY JOB

If you're reading this, chances are you've spent the last several weeks, months or even years trying to get hired into a full-time, salaried role. You've probably told yourself that things will eventually get better. That you'll figure something out. That you'll sit tight, adjust your resume a little, and wait for the market to turn. But the reality is hard to ignore: the longer you're out of a white-collar job, the harder it is to get back into the workforce. And the harder it is to live the kind of life you actually want to live.

Some people tell themselves they'll temporarily pivot to blue-collar work. But let's be honest, your body won't hold up. If you're over forty, the physical labor required for warehouse shifts, factory work, food service, or delivery driving is brutal. You're not twenty anymore. Your back knows it. Your knees know it. And the hours? They're relentless. Blue-collar labor doesn't come with ergonomic chairs, flexible work-from-home policies, or scheduled PTO. It's day in, day out, and it breaks you down fast. A blue-collar job is not a temporary fix; it's a fast track to injury and burnout.

Others try to escape the job market entirely. They look at their savings and think, *Maybe I can coast for a while.* But inflation doesn't care about your spreadsheets. The cost of living in the US has surged more in the past three years than in the previous ten combined.[2] Rent, groceries, insurance, utilities — everything is climbing. Your dollar is shrinking faster than you can cut expenses, and whatever cushion you've built is being eroded monthly by forces you can't control. Even if you've been frugal and even if you've planned ahead, the math just doesn't work. You can't out-budget the economy.

THE FANTASY OF SELF-EMPLOYMENT AS A WAY TO GET BY

Starting a consulting business. Launching a coaching practice. Picking up freelance gigs on the side. It sounds appealing to be your own boss, set your own hours, and charge what you're worth, but running a successful business isn't about how smart you are. It's about how many clients you can close. And client acquisition is the hardest part of any business.

Selling yourself, day in and day out, on platforms flooded with younger, cheaper, hungrier competitors from around the globe, is exhausting. It's also expensive. The cost of building a brand, running ads, and chasing contracts eats away at your margins and your sanity.

Even franchising, which is often marketed as a safer alternative to traditional entrepreneurship, is loaded with hidden traps. Franchise fees alone can run into six figures. And the fine print? It's filled with annual royalties, mandatory insurance policies, marketing obligations, and lock-in contracts that limit your flexibility and expose you to legal and financial risk. You don't really own the business; you just rent the right to manage someone else's system, and at a steep cost.

RETIREMENT WILL NOT SAVE YOU, AND NEITHER WILL THE GOVERNMENT

Retirement isn't an answer either, not unless you want to cut your lifespan short. One study published in the *British Medical Journal* found that individuals who retired at 55 were 89% more likely to die within 10 years than those who retired at 65.[3] Another, from Oregon State University, showed that people who delay retirement by just one year reduce their risk of death by 11%, regardless of health status.[4] The key takeaway from both of these studies is that work sustains life. Not just financially, but physically and mentally. Without structure, purpose, and income, decline sets in faster than most expect.

And if you're thinking you'll wait for the government to step in, don't hold your breath. Universal basic income, while a hot topic in policy circles, remains a distant dream. Pilot programs exist, but national implementation is years, if not decades, away. EBT benefits, meanwhile, are shrinking. States are quietly rolling back pandemic-era expansions, and eligibility rules are tightening. You may qualify for government support today and be dropped tomorrow. It's not a stable lifeline. It's a brittle string.

Even the systems that were built to support aging Americans, like Social Security, Medicare, and Medicaid, are stretched thin. According to the latest Congressional Budget Office projections, Social Security trust funds are on pace to be depleted by the mid-2030s. Medicare Part A isn't far behind. And as the funding disappears, so do your options. Fewer providers accept Medicare each year. Fewer clinics take Medicaid. Coverage gaps are growing. Co-pays are rising. And private supplemental insurance is increasingly unaffordable without employer backing.

HEALTHCARE IS A NECESSITY, AND SALARIED ROLES ARE THE GATEKEEPERS

In America, the single most reliable way to secure healthcare — real, comprehensive healthcare — is through a full-time job. Not a part-time role. Not gig work. Not a 1099. A full-time, salaried position with W-2 benefits. That's your entry ticket to stability. That's your access point for dental, vision, mental health, prescriptions, preventive care, and everything else you'll need more of, not less, over the next two decades. Without it, every doctor's visit becomes a negotiation. Every diagnosis becomes a threat to your savings. Every accident becomes a crisis.

You cannot afford to sit this out. You cannot afford to wait for something to "come along."

You have to get back into a high-quality role now. Not later. Now. Because the longer you remain out of the system, the harder it is to convince others — and yourself — that you belong in it. Gaps grow.

> **You cannot afford to sit this out. You cannot afford to wait for something to "come along."**

Relevance fades. Confidence erodes. And worst of all, you begin to lose access to the one thing that gives you leverage in this economy: your employability.

CHAPTER 3

START OVERCOMING THE OVERQUALIFIED PROBLEM WITH HIGH COMMITMENT

In our next meeting, Elaine slumped in her chair and said, "I applied to four more roles. We'll see."

"How badly do you actually want any of them?" I asked.

She gave a weak smile. "I'd take them."

That's when I told Elaine and Daniel about my parents losing their jobs when I was a pre-teen and their struggle to re-enter the workforce with jobs that were well-suited to their qualifications and decades of experience. That experience taught me that when you lose your job, everything else can fall apart. Keeping others from having the same experience as my parents is what makes my work feel so personal to me.

If you want to be taken seriously as a candidate today, especially if you're highly experienced, you need to signal one thing above all else: that you want *this* job, at *this* company, more than any other. You can't just sound enthusiastic on paper or during an interview; you need to remove all doubt that *this* is the job you want.

When hiring managers see someone with your credentials and career history, they assume you're browsing. Testing the waters. Looking for a temporary landing spot until something better comes along.

You may know that's not true. But they don't.

COMMITMENT IS THE FIRST AND MOST POWERFUL WAY TO OVERCOME THE OVERQUALIFIED LABEL

The *Journal of Personality and Social Psychology* study I shared in Chapter 1 found that even the most qualified candidates were viewed more positively and were more likely to be hired when they *demonstrated high levels of commitment to the specific job and company.* Not generic interest. Not professional courtesy. Real, observable, targeted commitment.

So how do you show that? You do it three ways:

1. Preparation
2. Positioning
3. Language

All three work together to shift the employer's perception of you from flight risk to first choice.

Hiring managers can tell when a candidate has done their homework, and for experienced professionals, preparation matters even more. You can't rely on your resume to do the convincing. You have to show them that you didn't just apply because the job matched a few keywords; you applied because you *chose* their company for a specific reason.

Before the interview, research the company deeply. Go beyond their home page and mission statement. Read investor updates, press releases, and LinkedIn posts from department leaders. Look for what they're struggling with, what they're expanding into, who their major clients are, and how the team is structured. Make it your job to understand their world.

Then, use that knowledge proactively. Reference something timely or specific in your cover letter or initial application. Mention a recent product launch or company initiative in your interview and tie it to your experience. Ask questions that show you've studied the company's evolution. Most applicants, especially younger or less experienced ones, won't go to this length. When you do, it makes an impression. It shows commitment before you even say the word.

STOP SAYING, "I'VE DONE THIS BEFORE."

Many overqualified candidates unintentionally undermine their own commitment by saying things like, "I've done this before," or "This would be a good transition for me," or "This is a solid fit with my background."

None of those statements signals loyalty. They signal neutrality. They say, "I can do this job," not "I want this job."

To keep from accidentally positioning yourself as someone who's just interviewing to collect a paycheck, you need to stop leading with what you've done and start leading with what you *want to do next*. That next thing? Make it clear that it's *this* role.

For example, you can say, "I'm looking to contribute long-term at a company where digital transformation is a priority. That's why I'm excited about this role." Or, "What draws me to this position is the way it combines strategic oversight with real operational impact. That's where I want to be."

Frame your past as preparation for this future, not as something you're trying to escape or downgrade. You're not taking this job because you're out of options. You're taking it because it's the *next* right one.

Recall that hiring managers responded most positively when candidates used clear, explicit statements of commitment. But in today's job market, it's not enough to show interest in the role; you have to show interest in *staying* in the role. Hiring managers aren't just looking to fill a seat. They're being judged, and in many cases, compensated, based on whether the person they hire will stay for *at least two years*. That's the standard retention key performance indicator. If you leave before that point, it reflects directly on them. If you stay for five years, ten years, or a career, it reflects positively on the hiring manager.

USE LONG-TERM LANGUAGE

Today's most sought-after candidates are those who don't just want a job; they want a future with the company. They don't say things like, "I'm exploring my options," or "This aligns with my skills." They say things like:

- "I'm looking for a company where I can commit long-term, and this is it."
- "This is the kind of role I see myself growing into over the next five, even 10 years."
- "I'm excited about the idea of building a long-term future here, not just contributing, but staying and evolving with the company."
- "If hired, I'll focus on making an impact now, but also on learning the business so I can support it long-term, wherever I'm needed."

These statements don't just project confidence; they de-risk you as a hire. They tell the hiring manager, "If you choose me, you won't have to go through this process again anytime soon."

And employers *will* test you on this. If your resume shows too many moves or any recent career gaps, expect them to ask questions like, "Where do you see yourself in five years?" or, "How does this role fit into your long-term goals?"

They're not asking to evaluate your ambitions. They're asking to evaluate your *loyalty*. What they want to hear is

START OVERCOMING THE OVERQUALIFIED PROBLEM WITH...

simple: "I see myself here. Doing what the company needs. Evolving with the team. Staying, contributing, and growing."

They want language that says, "This is not a temporary stop. This is where I plan to stay."

Long-term commitment is what builds trust. It's what gets you hired in a system that assumes people like you — someone experienced, overqualified, and resourceful — will walk away the minute something shinier comes along.

You have to take that assumption off the table. And once you do, everything starts to change.

If you had *fewer* qualifications, you wouldn't have to work this hard to prove your interest. But because you bring more to the table, you have to offset the assumption that you're only here temporarily, or worse, that you're settling. That's the price of being seen as "too good."

Fortunately, there's a silver lining to this whole situation. When you *do* signal high commitment as a high-capability candidate, the effect is stronger than it would be for someone with fewer credentials. You're no longer seen as risky; you're seen as rare. A top-tier professional who *wants* to be part of the team. That's compelling. That's powerful.

And that's when you start getting hired again.

In the next chapter, we'll move to the second essential adjustment: showing the hiring manager that you're organizationally aligned. Because once you've made it clear that you want to be there, the next question becomes whether you know how to *belong* there.

CHAPTER 4

ALIGN YOURSELF WITH THE COMPANY'S VALUES AND CULTURE

At the end of our first week of working together, Daniel handed me a version of his resume he'd tailored for one company.

The resume was flawless, except it still sounded like him.

"This doesn't sound like *them*," I told him.

Both Daniel and Elaine looked puzzled, so I reminded them how my parents thought their experience spoke for itself. They never learned to adapt their message. They never translated their value into the language employers wanted to hear, and the market punished them for it.

I watched my mom send out resumes with the same phrasing she'd used for years, only to hear nothing back. I watched my dad try to impress people with long lists of skills they didn't care about anymore. They didn't realize the rules had changed, and because they didn't adapt, we paid the price.

"When you're overqualified," I said, "you can't expect companies to meet you halfway. You have to meet them where they are, mirror their priorities, and reflect their values. You need to deeply embody their company culture in every interaction. If you don't, they'll never picture you on their team, no matter how perfect you are for the role."

THE HIRING SYSTEM REWARDS ALIGNMENT

If you've spent decades building expertise, leading teams, and making judgment calls, you've likely developed your own way of doing things. You've earned autonomy. You've learned to trust your instincts. And you've probably been told that your track record speaks for itself. But to the people hiring you now, that's not what matters most.

What matters is whether you'll *fit in* — with the company, with the team, and with the culture already in place. And that's not an abstract preference. It's a metric. A filter. A nonnegotiable requirement embedded into every Applicant Tracking System, every interview rubric, and every final hiring decision.

The science backs this up. As discussed in Chapter 1, researchers have found that high-capability candidates were far more likely to be hired when they showed strong *organizational orientation*, when they made it clear that their focus was on supporting the *company's* goals, not just advancing their own. Those who appeared self-focused, those who talked mostly about personal career growth, individual contributions, or past leadership, were rated less favorably, even if they were the most qualified people in the applicant pool.

In short, talent alone is not enough. You have to prove that your talent will integrate with a company's existing culture. This emphasis on cultural alignment is about managing risk just as much as it's about maintaining office harmony. Every hiring decision is a gamble. If the new hire doesn't work out, the company loses time,

> **Talent alone is not enough. You have to prove that your talent will integrate with a company's existing culture.**

money, and momentum. The easiest way to de-risk that decision is to hire someone who looks, talks, and acts like they already belong.

This is where highly experienced candidates often get penalized. You're different. You bring new ideas. You use different language. You reference older systems. You mention approaches the team hasn't heard of. That *should* be an asset, but in practice, it often feels unfamiliar. And unfamiliarity creates doubt.

When you're applying for a new position, your job is not to water down your experience. It's to translate it. To show that what you've done before will not only *fit* their culture, it will *strengthen* it.

SHOW FIT BY UNDERSTANDING THE CULTURE YOU'RE ENTERING

The first step to demonstrating cultural alignment is to understand the culture you're entering. That means going far beyond the company's mission statement or website. Every organization has an *actual* culture that exists beneath the slogans. Your job is to find it and then speak directly to it with your application and in interviews.

Start by reviewing online profiles about the company. Look for repeated language, phrases like fast-paced, collaborative, hierarchical, entrepreneurial, metrics-driven, and mission-first. Pay attention to what employees complain about and what they praise in online forums. Then, read what the company posts on LinkedIn. Look at how their leadership talks. How they celebrate wins. Whether they promote from within. Whether they focus on stability or disruption. These cues tell you what matters inside the organization, and how to mirror that in your messaging.

In interviews, align your language with theirs. If they're obsessed with data, talk about measurable outcomes. If they highlight teamwork, talk about how you support and mentor peers. If they care about fast decision-making, reference times you've led through ambiguity or scaled new systems quickly. Don't make the conversation about what *you* like; make it about how you've learned to succeed in environments like *theirs*.

For example:

- "In my last role, I worked in a fast-moving team where priorities shifted weekly. I learned how to stay flexible without losing focus, something I see is also important here."
- "I've been in both highly structured and entrepreneurial environments, but what I really enjoy is mission-driven work like what your team is doing."
- "I've led global teams, but I've found that the tight-knit, collaborative approach your company describes is where I do my best work."

These statements don't just show that you've done the work; they show that you've *done your homework*. They demonstrate self-awareness and adaptability — two of the most valuable traits in a new hire.

BE AN EAGER STUDENT

Another one of the biggest mistakes overqualified candidates make — especially in interviews — is unintentionally projecting superiority. It doesn't take much. A phrase like, "I've seen this before," or, "In my experience, we did it differently," can land wrong. It signals that you think your way is better. That you're already critiquing a system you haven't joined yet.

Instead, emphasize curiosity and humility. Employers want to know that you're ready to learn their way of doing things, not just teach your own. Even if you could run circles around the interviewer technically, that's not what they're evaluating. They're looking for someone who's coachable. Collaborative. Willing to integrate.

Say things like:

ALIGN YOURSELF WITH THE COMPANY'S VALUES AND CULTURE

- "I'm excited to learn how your team approaches this. I've seen a few methods, but I'm always refining mine."
- "Your strategy is something I want to get better at. It's part of why I'm so interested in this role."
- "I'm here to contribute, but also to listen and understand what's already working well for your team."

This kind of language doesn't erase your expertise; it makes it more *welcoming*.

You don't have to pretend to be someone you're not. You don't have to memorize the company's entire About page or fake enthusiasm for Ping-Pong tournaments or remote yoga sessions. Cultural alignment is about core values and behavior, not corporate perks or Hawaiian shirt day. It's about showing that you respect how the organization operates, and that you're willing to support its way of doing things, even if you bring a different perspective.

How you speak and position yourself during an interview is about building trust. And when you're considered overqualified, trust is the thing you have to earn first, before they can see everything else you bring.

In the next chapter, we'll explore how to address employers' fear that you're still looking around and that the job you're applying for is just one of many options you're entertaining. You'll learn how to position yourself as fully focused, fully committed, and ready to stay for the long haul, because that's the final key to getting hired when the system sees you as a risk.

CHAPTER 5

THIS ROLE IS YOUR TOP CHOICE, NOT JUST ONE OF MANY

The next day, Elaine came into my office clutching a posting for a company she genuinely loved. "This one's different," she said, her voice alive. She told me about their mission, their latest product, and their leadership team. She sounded nothing like the woman from our meeting last week.

"This," I said, "is how you should sound about every role you pursue."

She frowned. "It's exhausting to fake that."

"It's not about faking. It's about only going after roles where you can find this energy. If you can't, don't apply. If you can, make sure they feel it," I said.

I thought about my mom losing her confidence after she was pushed out of her career. She applied everywhere because she had to. But to employers, she was just another resume, someone who'd say yes to anything. As time passed, the rejections piled up and her self-esteem suffered, intensifying the cycle of pain.

"When you're overqualified," I told Elaine, "you have to make them believe they're your first choice. Companies want to feel chosen. If they don't, they choose someone else."

MAKE EVERY COMPANY YOU APPLY TO YOUR TOP CHOICE

If you want to get hired as a highly capable candidate, you have to stop looking like someone who's just browsing.

That's how most employers see you at first: like a shopper with too many options who's half-interested in what they're offering and likely to walk away at the last minute. It doesn't matter how enthusiastic you sound. If you're overqualified, experienced, or older, or if you have lots of education, employers will automatically assume you're only applying for the job as a backup plan, and the second something better comes along, you'll leave.

This fear is so deeply embedded in hiring culture that most employers never even realize they're acting on it. But they are. And unless you neutralize it, you'll keep getting rejected for roles you're perfectly qualified for, or worse, *because* you're perfectly qualified for them.

Fortunately, overqualified candidates are just as likely to be hired as other applicants, *if* they make it clear that the role in front of them isn't just acceptable, it's preferred. It's their *first choice*.

On the surface, it's easy to assume the way to combat a company's fear about your long-term commitment is with flattery. However, clearly expressing why this role is *the role* for you is about strategy. Employers are making bets. They're trying to predict who's going to stick around. And they know from experience that the candidates who seem ambivalent,

> **Fortunately, overqualified candidates are just as likely to be hired as other applicants, *if* they make it clear that the role in front of them isn't just acceptable, it's preferred.**

who talk vaguely about "next steps" or "broad interests," are the ones most likely to disappear when a shinier offer appears.

COMMUNICATE A SINGULAR FOCUS

So, if you want to get hired, you have to stop saying things like, "I'm exploring a few opportunities," or "I'm keeping an open mind." That may feel honest, but it sounds noncommittal.

Instead, you need to communicate a singular focus. Not desperation, but clarity. You're not here to *see* what's out there. You're here because you've already *seen* what's out there, and this is the opportunity that matters most.

Here's how that sounds:

- "I've had conversations with other companies, but your company is my top choice because it aligns with what I've been looking for."
- "I've spent time evaluating different types of roles, and this one checks every box for me."
- "If I'm fortunate enough to get this offer, I plan to stop interviewing elsewhere. This is where I want to invest."
- "This role isn't just a match for my background; it's a match for my long-term goals. That's why it's my top choice."

These statements are powerful because they reduce uncertainty. The hiring manager doesn't have to wonder whether you'll accept. They don't have to worry that you're stringing them along. They know where you stand. And that's exactly what they want.

Still, you'll need to be ready to prove it. Saying a role is your top choice isn't enough; you have to *show* why. That means connecting specific aspects of the job to your personal goals, values, and motivations in a way that feels intentional.

For example:

- "One thing that really appeals to me about this role is the opportunity to work cross-functionally. That's been a core part of what I've enjoyed most in past roles, and it's something I want to continue doing."
- "I've been following your company for a while, your work in X really stands out, and it aligns with what I care about professionally."
- "I'm at a point in my career where stability and contribution matter more than constant advancement. This team's mission and size feel like the right place for me to land and stay."

When you make these connections out loud, you invite the hiring team to picture you staying with them for the long haul. You create a narrative of continuity. A story they can believe in.

Unfortunately, even if you successfully convey why this company and role are what you want, the follow-up questions are where many candidates get caught. Employers are going to test whether this role is really your top choice. They'll ask questions like:

- "Where else are you interviewing?"
- "What would you do if you got another offer?"
- "What does your ideal role look like?"
- "Where do you see yourself in five years?"

Employers want to hear that you've thought it through. That you're not just running from something, you're running *toward* something. Specifically, *this*. And when they ask about five years from now, they don't want to hear about graduate school, starting a business, or climbing the ladder somewhere else. They want to hear that you see yourself at *their* company, helping *their* team, adapting to what's needed, and staying the course.

So, say it clearly:

- "In five years, I see myself here, doing what's needed to help the company succeed, whether that's growing in this role or taking on new challenges as they arise."
- "If I get this offer, I won't be pursuing other opportunities. This is the one I've been looking for."
- "This is not a placeholder role for me; it's one I want to invest in for the long-term."

You don't need to be theatrical. You just need to be specific. Because there is a cost to hedging.

Here's what you're up against: most candidates, especially those who are younger or less experienced, are willing to say anything to get the job. They'll overpromise, oversell, and say, "This is my dream job," without a second thought. But hiring managers know that overqualified candidates *don't* usually say those things. They expect you to be measured. Thoughtful. Careful. That's why, when you *do* say it, when you clearly state that this is the role you want, it stands out. It cuts through the noise. It shifts the balance.

It tells the employer: "You're not just choosing me. I've already chosen you." That's the most persuasive thing you can say in a system designed to reject people who seem like they have better options.

In the chapters ahead, we'll explore how to stop proving yourself out of a job, especially by rewriting your resume in a way that doesn't just pass through filters, but positions you as the committed, aligned, long-term hire every employer is secretly hoping to find.

CHAPTER 6

STOP PROVING YOURSELF OUT OF A JOB

After I finished talking to Elaine, Daniel leaned across the table, frustration in his voice. "I gave them everything — every result, every metric. I showed them I could hit the ground running on day one."

I shook my head slowly and said, "And that's why you lost."

He stared at me, confused. I told him about how, after losing his job, my dad went into every interview with a desperate determination to prove himself. He'd unload his entire career in the first ten minutes — decades of achievements, numbers, systems improved. He thought he was making the decision easy for them. But what they saw was someone who might outshine them, challenge their authority, or leave as soon as something better came along.

"When you're overqualified," I told Daniel, "more proof can actually make you look like a bigger risk. You trigger fear instead of confidence. You make them question whether they can manage you, or if you'd even want the role long-term."

I made this mistake in my own career. I got one degree, then another, and another, thinking that each degree would make it easier to get hired. Somehow, it made it harder. Then

I got experience, and things became even harder. My achievements worked against me.

I leaned toward Daniel. "You don't need to hide your achievements," I said. "You need to reframe them to lead with your potential, not your proof."

Daniel tapped his pen nervously. "So... I shouldn't talk about my experience?"

"You should," I said, "but not as a history lesson. Frame it as a bridge to what you'll do for them next. The key is to start with the latter."

THE HARDER YOU TRY, THE MORE YOU PUSH THEM AWAY

You've done everything they told you to do. Earned the titles. Built the track record. Got the degrees. You've climbed the ladder rung by rung and have the results to prove it. And now, when it matters most, when you're applying to roles you could do in your sleep, no one's calling you back.

It doesn't make sense. But it happens every day. The proven candidate with years of experience, a glowing track record, and measurable results gets passed over. The lesser-known, less-accomplished, greener candidate gets the offer. The job. The promotion. The opportunity.

You've earned your stripes. But the hiring manager is more excited by someone who *might* be good than by your proof that you already are.

So, you double down. You try harder to sell yourself as the most qualified candidate. You list every accomplishment. You give detailed examples. You start interviews by describing how much responsibility you've handled, how many millions you've managed, how many people you've led. You think you're proving your value.

But that's the problem. You're not getting rejected

> You're not getting rejected *in spite of* your credentials. You're getting rejected *because* of how you present them.

in spite of your credentials. You're getting rejected *because* of how you present them.

The system isn't looking for proof anymore. It's looking for promise. And when you focus entirely on what you've done, you come across as someone who's already peaked. Someone who isn't open to growth. Someone who might be great but is finished becoming. That's not who employers want to hire.

Experience doesn't excite them, mystery does. It sounds ridiculous. But there's hard science behind it. As we'll explore more now and through the next chapter, peer-reviewed studies show that people are *more impressed* by potential than by achievement.[5] Not in theory. In real-world decision-making. Managers consistently offer more money, more praise, and more opportunity to candidates described as "high potential" than to those with identical, but proven, track records.

This means that the very thing you've been told to lead with — your resume of wins — is, in many cases, working against you.

THE POTENTIAL EFFECT IS WORKING AGAINST YOU

If you lead with sharing all your credentials, achievements, and personal wins, you're giving employers too much certainty. And certainty is boring. When evaluators are presented with someone who's already accomplished something, their brains stop processing. They accept the information and move on. But when they're shown someone *on the verge* of success, with all signs pointing upward, they keep thinking. They analyze more deeply. They unconsciously amplify the value of what that person *could* become.

In psychology, this is called *the potential effect*. And if you're overqualified, it's the one thing you can't afford to ignore. Overqualified candidates sabotage themselves. When experienced professionals try to prove themselves, they usually do three things:

1. They lead with history, past titles, past responsibilities, and past results.
2. They sound conclusive, and their tone says, "I've done it all," even if their words say, "I'm open to more."
3. They talk like consultants by solving problems, giving advice, and showing mastery.

To the employer, it feels like talking to someone who *should be on the other side of the table*. It creates distance. Intimidation. Discomfort.

That's when the quiet disqualification begins. You're not getting rejected because they think you can't do the job, but because they think you won't *want* to do the job once you see how small it is. Why would you? You've clearly already done bigger things.

By using this type of language in your applications, resume, and interviews, you're closing the book on yourself, and employers want a story that's still unfolding. Repositioning yourself as someone who is still growing is the way to overcome this problem. And while you shouldn't pretend to be inexperienced, you do need to create forward momentum in the way you talk about your career.

POTENTIAL IS MORE POWERFUL THAN PROOF

Another thing every overqualified job seeker needs to understand to survive this new hiring landscape is that potential beats proof every time.

The research about leading with potential is clear — and shocking. In a groundbreaking series of studies, researchers from Stanford and Harvard Business School uncovered a consistent and counterintuitive trend indicating that people don't just admire potential; they *prefer* it over actual achievement.[6]

In one experiment, evaluators reviewed two job candidates with nearly identical backgrounds. One had *demonstrated* leadership ability in a similar role. The other scored highly on a test of *leadership potential*. Despite acknowledging that the experienced candidate had the more impressive resume, hiring managers still ranked the potential-based candidate as more likely to succeed.

In another study, participants were asked to imagine they were NBA team managers evaluating a player. One group was told the player *had already* averaged impressive stats for five seasons. The other group was told the exact same stats were just *projections* of what the player *could* do in his first five years.

Participants were then asked, "What would you pay the player in year six?" The player with potential was offered nearly one million dollars *more* than the player with proven performance. He was also believed to be more likely to make the All-Star team and to become a franchise leader.

The same trend showed up in experiments involving artwork, restaurants, and even Facebook ads. In each case, people gravitated toward the *next big thing* over the *already big thing*.

The researchers carefully controlled for age, so before you think, *I'm too old for this data to apply to me,* think again. It wasn't about qualifications either. The only difference between candidates was the framing — proven versus possible. And over and over again, *possible* won.

POTENTIAL GETS EMPLOYERS EMOTIONALLY INVESTED

Hiring managers think, *This candidate already did something impressive, so I don't need to think much about them.* They've likely skimmed your credentials and already filed your application away.

But if a candidate *could* become impressive, the hiring manager stays engaged. They think, *I want to see what they could become. I think they might be great, and I want to see if my prediction will come true.* They get emotionally invested in you and your future potential with the company.

This is why companies are willing to pay more, take bigger risks, and roll the dice on unproven people if those people look like they're going somewhere. If they appear to be *becoming*.

If you're reading this book, you are the highly qualified, proven candidate. You've already succeeded. You've already built your credentials. You've already done what the other applicant *might* do someday. But if you present yourself that way, if you come across as a finished product, you're going to lose. The way to counteract this perception is to talk about what you *want to do next* and paint a clear picture of your growth trajectory. To talk like someone who is still climbing.

COMMUNICATE YOUR POTENTIAL

How do you position yourself as high potential at any age? Start by speaking in the future tense. Talk about what excites you *next*, not what satisfied you before.

Say things like:

- "I'm excited about applying what I've learned to new challenges."
- "What motivates me now is the chance to grow in this area."
- "I see this role as the next chapter, not the last."

Then, build anticipation. Don't just summarize what you've done, frame it as preparation:

- "The last few years taught me how to lead through complexity. Now I want to go deeper into cross-functional innovation."
- "I've delivered consistent results in structured environments, and I'm ready to contribute in a space that values agility and learning."

EXAMPLES OF PAST-FOCUSED VERSUS POTENTIAL-FOCUSED LANGUAGE

Let's extend this concept of potential-focused language to how you should be writing the bullet points in your resume.

Resumes will be covered in full in Chapters 16 and 17, but let's start thinking about how you can shift the language in your resume to shift a hiring manager's perception of you from "over the hill" to "on their way up."

At best, most highly qualified candidates try to prove themselves by only listing what they've accomplished in their past:

- Aligned reporting frameworks across departments and reduced decision cycle times by 35%.
- Managed 4 dashboards and predictive models that supported $60M in vendor deals.
- Orchestrated multi-market data alignment between business partners by following company protocols to increase compliance rates by 42%.

You likely read the bullet points above and thought they read perfectly fine. You may have even thought, *Wow, these are better than my own bullet points*, because they included hard numbers.

Metrics, in the form of numerical values (*10*, not *ten*), are mandatory additions to each resume bullet point given how today's artificial intelligence (AI)-driven Applicant Tracking System (ATS) resume filters score. We will be covering that in detail in future chapters, including how these systems give you, the job candidate, a reputation score.

Now, consider these example resume bullet points that discuss a candidate's potential only:

- Poised to lead cross-functional business intelligence initiatives, building on a foundation of collaborative analytics across departments.
- Positioned to maintain team alignment on data strategy projects in emerging markets and technologies by expanding on advanced analytics expertise.
- Ready to take on scaling global communications by bringing internal teams together.

Most overqualified job candidates will read the bullet points above and believe they sound weaker than the previous three bullet points. But, as the Stanford and Harvard researchers demonstrated, this belief is wrong. Employers prefer potential over proof when hiring.

Yet, proof still matters — as mentioned, you must include hard numbers to support your claims — but the key is including them in the right order, after your potential statements.

Here are examples of how you can effectively lead with potential and close the loop with proof backed by numerical values:

- Poised to lead cross-functional business intelligence initiatives, building on a foundation of collaborative analytics across departments, as previously demonstrated by aligning reporting frameworks and reducing decision cycle times by 35%.
- Positioned to maintain team alignment on data strategy projects in emerging markets and technologies by expanding on advanced analytics expertise, as shown by successfully managing 4 dashboards and predictive models that supported $60M in vendor deals.
- Ready to take on scaling global communications by bringing internal teams together and helping orchestrate multi-market data alignment between business partners by following company protocols, as evidenced by increasing compliance rates by 42%.

Structuring your resume bullet points to lead with potential supported by data means you can still bring the receipts, you're just not focusing on the past.

You don't have to pretend to be less experienced. This isn't about dumbing yourself down or hiding your credentials. It's about showing that your *story isn't over yet.* You're not proving your worth, you're projecting it forward.

That's the real pivot. Employers are afraid of hiring someone who's "done." They want someone with momentum.

Someone they can bet on. Someone who, if nurtured, will do their best work *here*, not just *somewhere else, years ago*.

So be that person. Frame your success as a foundation, not a finale. Speak in terms of growth, not closure. Make them believe that if they hire you now, the best is yet to come. Because that's how you turn your overqualification from a threat into a promise.

CHAPTER 7

LEAD WITH POTENTIAL, ANCHOR WITH RESULTS

At the end of our first week working together, Daniel handed me a printed copy of his new professional summary — three paragraphs of nothing but metrics. "They'll have to take me seriously when they see this," he said.

I read the first few lines, then crossed most of them out. In their place, I wrote: Ready to lead high-impact projects in operations strategy, leveraging a track record of improving efficiency by 32% over 5 years.

"See the order?" I asked. "Potential first, results second."

"When you lead with potential, the hiring manager starts imagining you in the role before they even think about your past," I explained. "Once they've mentally hired you, your results become the clincher."

IT'S NOT ALL ABOUT RESULTS, BUT RESULTS STILL MATTER

You can't just prove yourself anymore. But you also can't just posture. This is the paradox facing every highly qualified job seeker: you're expected to show potential, not just performance, but you're also expected to be credible, trustworthy, and real. Hiring managers want candidates who are ready for the next level, not ones who are resting on the last one. But they also want proof that those candidates can deliver.

The solution is balance. Not a watered-down compromise, but a strategic sequencing. You start with potential. You lead with momentum toward the future. You open the door with what's next. And then, you walk them through it with the right past performance to back it up.

> **You open the door with what's next. And then, you walk them through it with the right past performance to back it up.**

It's not just what you say, it's how you structure it. Think about the difference between these two statements:

- Managed a $2M cross-functional project across 3 global teams.
- Poised to lead high-impact global initiatives, building on cross-functional success, as demonstrated by managing a $2M project across 3 teams.

The first statement is impressive. It's clear, concrete, and verifiable. But it's rooted entirely in the past. The second is dynamic. It positions the speaker as someone in motion, someone on their way up, and uses results as fuel for what's next.

The first closes a loop. The second opens one. And in today's hiring market, open loops — potential-based phrases — win.

LANGUAGE THAT SIGNALS POTENTIAL

In the previous chapter, we explored the scientific preference for potential over proof. The studies by Tormala, Jia, and Norton showed that people, hiring managers included, respond more positively to candidates described as having *room to grow* than to those described as already accomplished.

To do this, you need to use language that positions you as ascending. That frames your story as evolving. That gives hiring managers the chance to *believe in you*, not just *verify you*.

Phrases like:

- Ready to take on...
- Poised to lead...
- On track to expand...
- Equipped to evolve into...
- Positioned to grow into...

These phrases suggest trajectory. They hint at future value. They encourage investment. They allow the employer to see you as a smart bet.

But they can't stand alone.

BACKING UP POTENTIAL WITH PROOF IN WORDS

Potential without evidence feels flimsy. Aspirational. Worse, it feels risky. Which is why you always follow potential-based language with proof and language that validates your promise.

This is where transitional phrases matter. Instead of dropping a bullet point, you embed a story. You tie it together. You show the link.

Use phrases like:

- As demonstrated by...
- As evidenced through...
- As shown by...
- Proven by...
- Previously exemplified through...

These transitions create continuity. They build trust. They turn your pitch from a resume recital into a coherent narrative. You're not just saying you can do something, you're showing why it makes sense for you to do it next.

This is the structure that allows overqualified candidates to sidestep the fear that they're "done," while also avoiding the trap of sounding too abstract:

1. **Start with potential**: Show you're moving forward.
2. **Transition to proof**: Show why that future is realistic.
3. **Close the loop with credibility**: Use measurable results to anchor belief.

For example:

- Poised to take on enterprise-level transformation initiatives by combining strategic foresight with operational acumen, as demonstrated by executing a compliance overhaul that reduced audit findings to zero across three inspections.
- Equipped to lead high-growth cross-functional teams in dynamic markets, previously demonstrated by guiding a 6-person unit that secured $1.8M in funding through competitive proposal writing.

It's a small shift. But for hiring managers, it makes all the difference because you're no longer just experienced, you're *investable*.

When making these changes to your resume language, it's important to avoid these two extremes overqualified candidates tend to drift toward:

1. **The Historian.** Every bullet point is a past-tense brag. It's heavy, impressive, and final.
2. **The Visionary.** Everything is about aspiration. It sounds fresh but lacks grounding.

Unfortunately, neither candidate gets hired.

Who does? The hybrid. The candidate who speaks from experience but signals momentum. The one who creates a bridge between their past value and their future potential.

LEAD WITH POTENTIAL, ANCHOR WITH RESULTS

It's the candidate who says:

- "I've built systems that work. I'm ready to build the next ones that scale."
- "I've delivered results. Now I'm prepared to deliver transformation."

Hiring is a risky decision, which means your job is to de-risk yourself as a candidate and excite your potential employer. Every manager is betting on someone. Your job is to make that bet feel smart. That means reducing perceived risk (with proof) while increasing perceived upside (with potential).

> **Every manager is betting on someone. Your job is to make that bet feel smart. That means reducing perceived risk (with proof) while increasing perceived upside (with potential).**

CHAPTER 8

LEARN TO BE AGREEABLE

Elaine sighed and said, "I thought I nailed it. We got along so well...then, nothing."

"How much did you smile?" I asked.

She blinked. "I was professional."

"Were you agreeable though?" I asked.

"Well...for the most part, I think. But I wanted to challenge their thinking on a few points," she said.

"Interviews today, especially early rounds, aren't a debate," I said. "They're an audition for cultural fit. When you're overqualified, you have to prove you can work inside their world before you try to change it."

Elaine's shoulders slumped. I said, "Next time, show curiosity. Ask how they do things and why. Agree on the fundamentals before you introduce your ideas."

The truth most overqualified candidates are never told is that when the hiring manager is already worried you might not fit in, likability isn't optional; it's essential. Employers hire those they like — even over more qualified candidates. In fact, one report found that candidates who received a job offer were 12 times more likely to be described as having a "great personality" than those who were rejected.[7]

Your level of likability answers the hiring manager's unspoken question: *Will I want to work with you every day?*

My mom carried herself with such guarded dignity after losing her job. She was polite in interviews, but cautious, almost defensive. I know now it was because rejection after rejection had worn her down. But this attitude was an immediate barrier to employers seeing her as a positive addition to their team. Unfortunately, this experience wasn't unique to my mother. Many of the highly qualified professionals I work with today have the same attitude during the interview process, whether they know it or not.

"When you're overqualified," I told Elaine, "you're a bigger question mark than the other candidates. Will you stay? Will you respect their leadership? Will you adapt? Likability erases those doubts. It gives you a competitive advantage."

I leaned forward. "The next time you interview, go in like you already belong. Smile. Share moments of connection. Showcase yourself as a collaborator, compromiser, and someone who brings alignment, peace, and calm. Be likable and be steady."

You've probably been told your whole life that competence is what counts. That hard work, results, and credentials will speak for themselves. And maybe for most of your career, that was true. But something has shifted, and now you're doing everything right, tailoring your resume, practicing interview answers, following up professionally, and still getting ghosted.

This rejection doesn't make sense until you understand that today's hiring decisions are evaluating what you've done *and* who you seem to be.

When you're sitting face-to-face with a hiring manager, the personality trait that matters most isn't ambition or intelligence. It's agreeableness.

AGREEABLENESS IMPROVES WORKPLACE OUTCOMES

A groundbreaking study titled "Agreeableness and Its Consequences: A Quantitative Review of Meta-Analytic Findings" analyzed over 1.9 million participants across nearly 4,000 studies.[8] It found that agreeableness, defined as kindness, trustworthiness, empathy, and cooperativeness, had positive effects in 93% of measured outcomes across the workplace, including job performance, interpersonal relationships, and psychological well-being.

These are the exact factors that determine who gets hired, who gets promoted, and who survives layoffs. In other words, agreeableness is no longer just a nice-to-have. It's a leading indicator of professional success.

And yet, most overqualified candidates have been trained to deprioritize agreeableness. You were told to be results-driven. You were encouraged to challenge assumptions, defend your ideas, and push back when things didn't make sense. You built a career on asking hard questions and demanding evidence. But what works in high-stakes environments or intellectual circles can backfire during job interviews, especially when employers are looking for signs of humility, flexibility, and cultural fit.

You might think you're being honest or efficient. But they're interpreting your approach as resistance. As someone who might be difficult to manage. As someone who won't adapt.

AGREEABLENESS PREDICTS PREDICTABILITY

A second study, "Kill Chaos with Kindness," drives this point home. It found that agreeableness isn't just about personality, it's about perceived predictability.[9] Agreeable people reduce uncertainty in chaotic environments. They calm teams. They create cohesion. In a world still recovering from massive economic instability, companies are desperate for that type of predictability.

Employers don't want candidates who create more friction. They want ones who bring stability. The study shows that in uncertain conditions, teams rally around people who demonstrate empathy, calm communication, and social alignment. That's not just good for morale, it directly improves performance.

Here's where it gets even more important for you as an overqualified candidate: the same traits that made you stand out in the past as the most suited for the job may now be making you stand out for the wrong reasons because you're seen as unpredictable.

You've had a long career, maybe even held leadership roles. You might come across as someone who won't take direction, or worse, someone who will try to take over. That's the perception you have to fight, not by hiding your experience, but by softening your signal. By demonstrating, through words and tone and presence, that you're here to contribute, not compete. That you're here to stay, not shake things up. This is why positioning yourself as a challenger, disruptor, or even innovator can backfire.

Recall from Chapter 7 when I shared how employers hire for uncertainty in the context of potential and how tapping into your limitless potential as a human can help you get hired. This type of potential-based uncertainty is not what I'm talking about here. Employers don't want uncertainty when they're thinking about whether or not you'll get along with your coworkers, fit into their culture, and do what you're told to do by superiors. In this realm, they want extreme certainty. Or put another way, very high levels of predictability.

HOW EMPLOYERS USE THE BIG FIVE PERSONALITY TRAITS

Psychologists call agreeableness one of the Big Five personality traits.[10] Today's AI hiring systems rely on this psychological model, which includes:

1. **Openness to Experience:** Curiosity, imagination, willingness to learn new things.
2. **Conscientiousness:** Organization, reliability, goal-orientation.
3. **Extraversion:** Sociability, enthusiasm, assertiveness.
4. **Agreeableness:** Kindness, empathy, cooperation.
5. **Neuroticism:** Emotional instability and negative affect, tendency to experience distress, mood swings, and worry.

Why these five? Because they've been validated across decades of peer-reviewed psychology research. Companies can claim, with legal confidence, that profiling job candidates using these traits is not arbitrary or biased. In fact, they consider it science-backed and compliant with current employment law. These models have been trained on tens of millions of data points, and they're not going away. In fact, they're being scaled by AI filtering systems, which we'll discuss in depth in Section 3.

The origins of the Big Five date back nearly a century. In the 1930s and 40s, psychologists Gordon Allport and Henry Odbert began cataloging thousands of adjectives used to describe human behavior, laying the groundwork for trait-based personality theory. Raymond Cattell later narrowed these down into 16 core factors using factor analysis, an early step toward the Big Five structure. In the 1960s, Air Force researchers Ernest Tupes and Raymond Christal identified five recurring factors in personality data that closely resemble today's Big Five traits. Their work, though largely overlooked at the time, became foundational.

In the 1980s, the model really gained traction. Lewis Goldberg coined the term "Big Five" in 1981, and Robert McCrae and Paul Costa developed the NEO Personality Inventory in 1985, which formalized the measurement of the five traits. Their research brought academic legitimacy and psychometric rigor to the model. From the 1990s onward, the Big Five became the dominant personality framework in psychology, organizational behavior, and, more recently, in machine learning applications like hiring algorithms. Its validity has been replicated in cross-cultural contexts and across multiple industries, making it an appealing foundation for algorithmic decision-making today.

Having a high level of agreeableness doesn't mean you're weak or a pushover. It means you know how to read a room and can adjust your tone, listen, and respond with warmth and flexibility. It means you're easy to work with, and in a job market flooded with fear, burnout, and overstretched managers, that's become one of the top hiring priorities.

In fact, the "Agreeableness and Its Consequences" meta-analysis we discussed previously found that agreeableness outperformed nearly every other personality trait when it came to predicting things like job performance, collaboration, lower turnover, and reduced counterproductive behavior. Why? Because agreeable people make organizations function more smoothly. They solve problems faster. They're trusted. They fit in. And they stay. For overqualified candidates, who are already viewed with suspicion, this trait becomes your secret weapon. When you combine a strong track record with the ability to make people feel at ease, you become someone worth fighting for.

But that's the problem, isn't it? Many highly experienced professionals have been trained, rewarded, and even promoted for being direct, analytical, and even critical. You've been in rooms where calling out problems earned you respect. You've led teams where pushing hard was necessary. But in today's job market, that edge is misread. That confidence is seen as inflexibility. That experience is mistaken for ego. Hiring managers don't want friction. They want compatibility. They want to know you'll follow before you lead. That you'll take direction. That you'll integrate, not dominate.

BE RELATIONAL, NOT TRANSACTIONAL, DISRUPTIVE, OR DOMINANT

So, what does agreeableness look like in practice? First, lead with relational language, not transactional language.

Relational Language	**Transactional Language**
I'd love to be part of a team like yours.	This position matches my skillset.
I'm excited to learn your systems.	Here's how I've done it before.

Second, mirror the tone of your interviewers. If they're warm and conversational, don't be rigid or clipped. Match their energy and make it easy for them to picture working with you.

Third, emphasize loyalty, stability, and collaboration. These are the signals of agreeableness, and they lower the unconscious barriers employers might have about your age, experience level, or perceived cost.

You don't have to lose your edge. You don't have to pretend to be someone you're not. But you do have to adjust your approach.

Start noticing how often you interrupt or dominate the conversation. Start reflecting back the language your interviewers use. Start emphasizing phrases like "happy to support," "eager to collaborate," "open to feedback," and "ready to learn your process." These phrases are psychological signals that tell employers you are adaptable, dependable, and not here to fight them, but to join them.

It's important to remember not to confuse agreeableness with weakness. The data doesn't support that. In fact, agreeable people are less likely to engage in toxic behaviors, more likely to stay with a company long-term, and more likely to create lasting value. This quieter kind of leadership listens first, joins second, and contributes steadily. It's the kind of presence hiring managers are starving for but don't know how to ask for directly.

If you're overqualified, agreeableness is your advantage. Because no matter how much experience you have, no one wants to work with someone who makes things harder. They want someone who makes the team feel whole. Someone who makes the decision easy. Someone who's not just qualified, but also likable. And that's not something you're born with. It's something you can choose to project every time you step into the room.

CHAPTER 9

SIX AGREEABLE STATEMENTS TO GET YOU HIRED

After we finished our conversation about her interview, I slid a piece of paper toward Elaine. On it, I'd written six phrases:

1. That's a great question.
2. I'd love to learn more about that.
3. I can definitely adapt to that.
4. That sounds like an exciting challenge.
5. I appreciate you sharing that.
6. I can see how that would work here.

"These aren't filler phrases you can use when a conversation lags," I told her. "They're micro-signals that lower the perceived risk of hiring you."

I remembered the last interviews I'd done when I was looking to make a mid-career change. I felt like I had arrived, and I wanted to show it. My interview answers were sharp and correct — and closed off. I failed to create openings for connection and gave no verbal cues that I could fit into someone else's system. The result? I had to interview for dozens of positions before getting hired.

"When you use statements like those on the paper in front of you," I told Elaine, "you're telling the employer you're safe to hire. That you'll meet them halfway. And when you're overqualified, that's the bridge that gets you to yes. Employers hire the person they feel they can work with, not just the one who can do the job."

As I shared in the previous chapter, agreeableness is not just a vibe. It's a set of phrases, statements, and conversational habits that can instantly signal that you're someone a company can bring on without fear.

Here are six high-impact statements you can use to shift how employers see you from risky to reliable, from intimidating to indispensable.

1. I AM A TEACHABLE INDIVIDUAL WHO IS EASY TO CORRECT AND INSTRUCT.

On the surface, this first statement might seem like a line better suited for someone just starting out in their career. But for you, someone with years, maybe decades, of experience, it's a signal that you don't carry ego into new environments. Hiring managers often assume that someone who's been a director, a professor, or a senior scientist will resist change or disregard the company's way of doing things.

This phrase neutralizes that fear. It tells them that you're adaptable. That you can enter a new system without disrupting it. That you'll listen before you lead. In short, it tells them you're safe to hire.

2. I AM AN AGREEABLE INDIVIDUAL.

This second statement may sound obvious, but most overqualified candidates never say it because they assume their professionalism or resume speaks for itself. But in today's market, people are looking for personality traits that make their lives easier.

Agreeable means drama-free. It means cooperative. It means you're not going to challenge every decision or bring emotional friction into the workplace. For someone with advanced credentials, this line is a shield; it tells the employer, "I'm not here to take over. I'm here to join your team." And in a flooded job market, that distinction matters more than a list of achievements ever will.

> **Agreeable means drama-free. It means cooperative. It means you're not going to challenge every decision or bring emotional friction into the workplace.**

3. I WILL WORK HARD TO COMPLETE THE GIVEN ASSIGNMENT.

The third statement is not flashy, but it's effective. In an era where many candidates flake, ghost, or treat jobs as disposable, this line tells the hiring manager exactly what they want to hear: you will follow through.

For highly educated candidates who may be seen as theory-heavy or results-removed, this phrase grounds your value in action. It says you're not just smart, you're dependable. That matters more than people realize. Reliability is the true differentiator in most roles. And this phrase delivers that message without having to spell it out.

4. YOU WON'T NEED TO TELL ME TWICE WHAT TO DO.

This fourth statement signals learning agility. It tells the employer that you're efficient, responsive, and low maintenance. It also subtly communicates that your experience won't be a barrier to direction and that you won't resist feedback or instructions.

Overqualified candidates are often seen as potential micromanagers or second-guessers. This line flips that script. It reframes your background as an asset because you've seen enough to understand quickly. Essentially, you won't need everything explained to you three times before you finally take action. And that makes you look like someone who would make your manager's job easier. Which, at the end of the day, is what most hiring managers are truly after.

5. I WANT TO WORK AT YOUR COMPANY BECAUSE...

This fifth statement is personal. As I said in Chapter 5, too many overqualified candidates make the mistake of treating the company like a fallback option. Their language is vague. Their answers are noncommittal. They seem like they're just looking for a paycheck or a temporary landing spot.

Hiring managers want someone who's chosen them. Someone who's done their homework. Someone who has a real reason to be there. When you follow this phrase with a specific, authentic reason for applying for the position, you demonstrate loyalty, focus, and genuine interest. You move from being a wildcard to a candidate they can picture long-term. That's how you pass the flight-risk filter that knocks out so many experienced applicants.

6. I HAVE SOLVED SIMILAR PROBLEMS. FOR EXAMPLE...

The sixth and final statement bridges potential with proof. As discussed in Chapters 6 and 7, leading with potential shows that while you're adaptable and easy to work with, you're also equipped to deliver results. It turns abstract qualifications into tangible value.

This is especially powerful if your background is technical; it gives the hiring manager a story they can remember, a situation they can relate to, and an outcome they can picture repeating. It's also a great opportunity to subtly steer the conversation toward your strengths while keeping the focus on their needs. You're not bragging. You're connecting.

AGREEABLENESS IS A STRATEGIC NECESSITY

Together, these six statements are strategic tools that help you shift the power dynamic in an interview. As I've said before, I'm not recommending you pretend to be less than you are, but I do recommend framing your strengths in a way that builds trust.

In a market that's oversaturated and increasingly skeptical of overqualification, these are the phrases that move you from the maybe pile to the shortlist. So, use them. Say them out loud. Practice them until they feel natural. Feeling comfortable using these phrases during an interview might just be the thing that gets you hired.

CHAPTER 10

THERE IS NO PERFECT JOB, BUT THERE IS THE RIGHT ONE FOR YOU

Daniel sat across from me, frowning at a printed job posting. "I could do this one with my eyes closed," he said, "but the location's a bit off. And the salary's about fifteen percent lower than I want."

I leaned back in my chair and said, "Daniel, you're chasing a fantasy job. The perfect role doesn't exist — at least, not one that checks every single box exactly when you need it to. And waiting for it is costing you time and momentum."

He bristled. "So, I should settle?"

"No," I said. "You should prioritize. Decide what matters most right now — stability, career progression, location, impact — and focus on finding a role that fits your current season of life."

I knew from personal experience watching my parents and having spent decades coaching professionals and helping them find employment that passing on good roles because they weren't perfect was not a winning strategy. The market moves on, options shrink, and sooner or later, that stress eats away at you.

"There's no perfect job," I said. "But there is the right job for you, right now. Take it, and you can reposition later." I could see the weight in his expression shift slightly — less frustration, more calculation. I could tell he realized this wasn't about lowering his standards but about playing the long game and keeping his career alive.

HOW TO CREATE A JOB SEARCH CRITERIA PRIORITIZATION MATRIX

When you've spent decades building a career, whether in business or leadership, starting a job search again can feel like being dropped into a maze without a map. You're not starting at zero, but the world has shifted beneath your feet.

Roles have changed. Expectations have changed. Even the definitions of *qualified* and *valuable* have changed. And although the perfect job might not exist for you right this moment, the right job for you right now absolutely does. You just need a new framework for finding it.

Most overqualified job seekers fall into one of two traps. Either you avoid the job search entirely because you're overwhelmed by fear, ego, or indecision, or you cast the widest possible net and apply to everything, hoping something sticks. Neither works. The first trap leads to paralysis. The second leads to exhaustion. In both cases, your search becomes reactive. And when you're overqualified, a reactive search only intensifies the biases

> **Most overqualified job seekers fall into one of two traps. Either you avoid the job search entirely because you're overwhelmed by fear, ego, or indecision, or you cast the widest possible net and apply to everything, hoping something sticks. Neither works.**

already working against you. You look unfocused. Desperate. Too senior for this, too expensive for that.

You can't afford to wander, which means you have to get clear about what features of a job are most important to you right now.

That's where the Job Search Criteria Prioritization Matrix comes in.

This matrix was created by Mimi Aboubaker and introduced in her Harvard Business Review article, "Finding a Job When You Don't Know What You Want to Do Next."[11] Think of it as a compass, not a checklist. It's not about finding the perfect job. It's about filtering out the wrong ones and fast-tracking the right ones before you waste time, energy, or reputation.

Here's how this matrix works. You start by evaluating six key categories:

1. Skills acquisition
2. Work environment
3. Long-term trajectory
4. Career narrative
5. Role type
6. Compensation

These categories force you to answer questions like what kind of environments make you better, not bitter? What are you willing to sacrifice and what's nonnegotiable? Are you looking for legacy, lifestyle, or leverage?

Once you've answered those questions, you rank each category by importance. Must-haves go to the top. Dealbreakers go to the bottom.

Maybe you've decided you'll never work under a micromanaging boss again. Maybe you're done with roles that offer prestige but no ownership. Maybe compensation isn't the most important thing anymore, but you still can't afford to take a pay cut. Whatever the case, the matrix helps you turn vague instincts into actionable filters. And for overqualified candidates, clarity is your best defense against being overlooked or misjudged.

HOW TO CREATE AN OPPORTUNITIES PRIORITIZATION MATRIX

Once you've created a hierarchy of which career category is most important to you, the search becomes surgical. You apply only to roles that meet your top criteria, and you disregard roles that violate your non-negotiables, even if they're tempting on the surface.

You can also begin to engage with your network more strategically, strategies for which we will discuss extensively in Chapter 25, The Hidden Power of Weak Ties and Workplace Alumni. To start, don't waste time on old colleagues who are just "willing to help." Instead, reach out to thought partners who understand your goals and opportunity-sourcers who are close to the roles you want. Introduce yourself with intention. Be direct about your transition. Own your experience, but position yourself as someone who's looking to contribute, not just command.

Once you start gathering opportunities, you can use Aboubaker's second tool, the Opportunities Prioritization Matrix. This one lets you compare roles based on your top two priorities, nothing more.

If you try to weigh everything, you'll never decide. The matrix gives you four quadrants: Focus Here, Be Mindful of Time Invested, Distractions, and Waste of Time.

Focus Here	**Be Mindful of Time Invested**
Distractions	**Waste of Time**

The only jobs worth pursuing seriously are those you've listed in the Focus Here quadrant. If a job doesn't deliver your top priorities, don't get seduced by shiny titles or familiar logos. That's how overqualified candidates end up stuck again, well paid, but underused and miserable.

YOU CAN'T HIT A TARGET YOU DON'T SET

A job search requires a target and a practical plan of execution. The old days of applying blindly and hoping your credentials speak for themselves are gone. Today's job market punishes ambiguity. The more qualified you are, the more intimidating you look, unless you show focus.

> Today's job market punishes ambiguity. The more qualified you are, the more intimidating you look, unless you show focus.

Structure your search around what you actually want, not just what you think you're allowed to ask for. That's not entitlement. That's strategy. You're not looking for a dream job. You're looking for a job that fits where you are now, that aligns with where you want to go next, and that lets you build something real, without having to shrink to get in the door.

CHAPTER 11

STOP SEARCHING JOB BOARDS, START FOLLOWING COMPANIES

Elaine scrolled through LinkedIn while we talked. "I check these twice a day," she said, "and still, there's nothing worth applying to."

I told her, "You're looking in the wrong place. Job boards are where opportunities go to die — or, at least, to get flooded with hundreds of applications."

She raised an eyebrow. "Then where are the good jobs?"

"Hidden," I said. "Up to eighty percent of senior roles aren't posted online. The people who get them already have relationships inside the company or are on the radar of hiring managers before the job is even official."

Daniel looked up from his computer and joined our conversation. "So, what do we do instead?"

"You stop chasing every public posting and start following companies directly on LinkedIn, in industry newsletters, and through alumni networks. You watch for headcount increases, leadership changes, product launches, and signs they might be hiring. Then you reach out before the listing ever goes up."

Elaine's scrolling slowed. "So, it's about being proactive instead of reactive?"

"Exactly," I said. "Job boards keep you playing catch-up. Following companies lets you be first in line. In a market where everyone's looking for reasons to screen you out, being early and known gives you a massive advantage."

THE GHOST-JOB EPIDEMIC PLAGUING OVERQUALIFIED CANDIDATES

There was a time when job boards were where jobs lived. But that time has passed. The modern job board is now little more than a legal checkbox for employers — a box they check to stay compliant, not to hire. And yet, most job seekers, especially those who are overqualified, still start their job search on job boards.

Using these lists to look for jobs wastes time, breeds discouragement, and positions you as one of 1,200 daily applicants fighting for a job that may not even be real. According to the *Wall Street Journal*, employers can now receive 1,200 applications or more per day for each job they post, up from 525 over several months just a few years ago.[12] That's not just a trend. It's a shift in power.

This shift has created an epidemic of ghost jobs — positions that are posted publicly but were never meant to be filled through public applications. A recent study from Resume Builder and featured on CBS News found that 3 in 10 job postings posted right now are ghost jobs, and that percentage is rising.[13] The number is worse for white-collar sectors where overqualified job candidates look the most. I've seen numbers as high as 8 out of 10 jobs listed being ghost jobs that employers have no intention of hiring for in the next six months, or at all. What a waste of time.

Employers know that just by listing a role on a job board, they'll get flooded with resumes. They also know they can mine those resumes later when another opening arises. Job boards today are now databases, not funnels. The jobs listed are simply placeholders because the hiring has already happened elsewhere. And where is that elsewhere?

Hiring is happening on LinkedIn, in company newsletters, on X, in Slack communities, and via email referrals. It's happening in quiet conversations and fast-moving threads. The real job market has moved. It's not on Indeed. It's in your feed.

> **Job boards today are now databases, not funnels. The jobs listed are simply placeholders because the hiring has already happened elsewhere.**

This is especially critical for overqualified job seekers. The more impressive your resume is, the more likely you are to be filtered out of job board pipelines by AI systems designed to spot flight-risk or over-experience markers. You can't wait for job boards to work in your favor — they won't. You need to change where and how you look for work. You need to stop searching job boards and start following companies.

GAIN CLARITY BY ELIMINATING OPTIONS

Like the process of using the Job Search Criteria Prioritization Matrix I shared in the last chapter, you don't need to search every job at every company. Instead, pick two or three sectors you genuinely want to work in. Then build a list of 30 to 80 companies within those sectors that you can track. Once you have that list, go to LinkedIn and start watching. Not their job boards, their headcount trends.

LinkedIn lets you see how many people have joined or left a company over the past month. If the number of employees has gone up, that's a sign the company is hiring externally. If it hasn't, or if you see a spike in internal promotions, the odds are good that any job they post publicly is already spoken for. In other words, they're posting for compliance.

Once you identify the companies with growing headcounts, follow them. Literally. Hit the follow button on LinkedIn. Subscribe to their newsletters. Watch what they post in their feeds. When they announce a role organically — a real job, with real urgency — it won't come through a job board. It will show up in a post, a press release, or an employee referral campaign. This is where you need to strike.

When companies post this way, they're not looking for hundreds of applicants. They're looking for the few who are paying attention. If you're watching, ready, and already understand the company's mission and recent news, you will stand out. You'll be one of the few people applying when the job is fresh and real, not one of 1,200 hoping to beat the algorithm.

THE MODERN JOB SEARCH IS COMPANY-CENTRIC,

Effective job searching today is proactive, not passive. It's built around relationships, relevance, and real-time responsiveness, not automated filtering and compliance-driven placeholders. If you're overqualified, you already know how the system works.

The question is whether you're willing to stop playing a game that's been rigged against you. The job boards are ghosts. The real opportunities are alive and visible, but only to those who follow where the jobs actually live.

SECTION TWO

SET A TARGET AND POSITION YOURSELF AS THE SAFE CANDIDATE

CHAPTER 12

CHOOSE SECTORS FIRST, NOT JOB TITLES

After discussing job boards with Elaine, I started reviewing Daniel's most recent resume submissions. He was hearing crickets back after applying and wanted to know why.

The problem? His resumes were all over the map. He was applying to wildly different job titles with no consistent theme and using a variety of different resume formats.

"You're sending mixed signals," I said. "Without a consistent narrative, no one knows what you're aiming for, and that makes you look unfocused."

Elaine leaned in. "But shouldn't we keep our options open?"

"Not like this," I said. "When you jump between titles across unrelated sectors, you dilute your brand. You need to pick two to three sectors where your skills are both in demand and relevant and then find the companies in those sectors that are hiring the most right now. Only then should you look at the job titles at those companies because job titles vary widely from one organization to the next."

I went on. "When you focus on sectors first, companies second, and then job titles, you become an insider candidate who has the best chance of getting an interview."

Daniel nodded slowly. "So, the title matters less than the company and sector?"

"Exactly." I nodded. "Sector first, company second, and title last. When you own your sectors and companies, you can pivot between roles without losing credibility. You stop looking like a desperate applicant and start looking like a strategic hire. Plus, you can negotiate job titles very easily once you're in front of a decision maker. But you have to get in front of them first."

Then, I asked Daniel and Elaine an important question: "Do either of you know what a North American Industry Classification System code — or NAICS — is?"

Confused, they looked at each other, and then at me, and said, "No."

"Don't worry," I said. "Most people don't know about this tool, but once you understand how these codes work, you'll have a much easier time finding an industry sector where you want to work."

Most job seekers, especially those who are overqualified, start their job search with themselves. They think, *What job title fits me? What skills do I want to use? What would I enjoy doing every day?* These aren't bad questions. But they're not the best place to start. Remember that your job search isn't about what's ideal in theory; it's about what's available in practice, as I shared in Chapter 10. And the jobs that are available don't start with your preferences. They start with sectors.

Sectors are how the business world is organized. They represent ecosystems of companies that solve related problems, sell related products, and follow related trends. When hiring increases in a sector, it increases across the companies inside it. That's where momentum happens. And that's where your job search should begin.

There are many ways to divide sectors. Financial analysts use categories like the S&P 500's 11 GICS sectors. Economists have their own models. But these frameworks are built for investors, not job seekers. They track stock performance, not hiring trends. For overqualified job candidates seeking white-collar roles, a better sector breakdown is one that reflects how modern companies are organized, how their teams scale, and where their needs create recurring demand for strategic hires.

WHICH NAICS CODES ARE RIGHT FOR YOU?

The North American Industry Classification System (NAICS) is the master index of the US economy. Every company you can think of, from a local dentist's office to a global manufacturer, sits inside this system. Each company gets a six-digit code that identifies its sector, subsector, industry group, industry, and its specific US industry.

At the highest level there are 20 sectors. Here are the sector titles and numbers:

1. Agriculture, Forestry, Fishing, and Hunting (11)
2. Mining, Quarrying, and Oil and Gas Extraction (21)
3. Utilities (22)
4. Construction (23)
5. Manufacturing (31-33)
6. Wholesale Trade (42)
7. Retail Trade (44-45)
8. Transportation and Warehousing (48-49)
9. Information (51)
10. Finance and Insurance (52)
11. Real Estate and Rental and Leasing (53)
12. Professional, Scientific, and Technical Services (54)
13. Management of Companies and Enterprises (55)
14. Administrative and Support and Waste Management and Remediation Services (56)
15. Educational Services (61)
16. Health Care and Social Assistance (62)
17. Arts, Entertainment, and Recreation (71)
18. Accommodation and Food Services (72)
19. Other Services (except Public Administration) (81)
20. Public Administration (92)

Every sector branches into subsectors, industries, and US industries. That branching structure is where your job search gets powerful because you can use NAICS codes to map out companies you never knew existed.

For example, say you recently applied to a Director of Operations role at H&M clothing. You can ask an AI platform like ChatGPT or Perplexity: *What is the NAICS code for H&M clothing?*

Instantly, you'll learn that H&M is classified under 448140: Family Clothing Stores.

By also asking, *What does each of these numbers mean for this company?* You'll find out that rolls up into the code hierarchy:

- Sector: 44-45 (Retail Trade)
- Subsector: 448 (Clothing and Clothing Accessories Stores)
- Industry Group: 4481 (Clothing Stores)
- Industry: 44814 (Family Clothing Stores)
- US Industry: 448140 (Family Clothing Stores)

Now you can take the code — 448140 — and use it as a key for numerous other prompts. For example, your next prompt could be: *What are other companies with NAICS 448140?*

Results will include Lands' End, Abercrombie & Fitch, Uniqlo, Gap, Levi Strauss, Guess, and Hugo Boss. Suddenly, you've gone from one target company to an entire ecosystem of peers.

USE NAICS CODES TO FIND JOBS WITH THE RIGHT LOCATIONS, CAREER TRACKS, AND MORE

Let's say you recently applied to an executive role at Cisco Systems and found out the primary NAICS code for the job is 334118: Computer Terminal and Other Computer Peripheral Equipment Manufacturing, and the job's overall code hierarchy is:

- Sector: 33 (Manufacturing)
- Subsector: 334 (Computer and Electronic Product Manufacturing)
- Industry Group: 3341 (Computer and Peripheral Equipment Manufacturing)
- Industry: 33411 (Computer and Peripheral Equipment Manufacturing)
- US Industry: 334118 (Computer Terminal and Other Computer Peripheral Equipment Manufacturing)

When you look for other companies in this code, you'll see Juniper Networks, IBM, Palo Alto Networks, NCR, Diebold Nixdorf, Xerox, Lexmark, Zebra Technologies, Fortinet, Honeywell Scanning & Mobility, and more.

Want to make it even more relevant? If you're using ChatGPT or another AI tool to help you search for jobs, you can use a prompt like this: *List 10 companies with NAICS 334118 within 50 miles of Houston, TX.*

You'll surface companies like Katron Technologies, Rose Electronics, and Peripheral Computer Support — names you'd never find scrolling job boards. And there's no limit to this rabbit hole. You can keep opening up new opportunities for yourself with further prompts, such as:

- List all companies in NAICS 713210 (Casinos) in Nevada.
- List the 20 largest companies in NAICS 221115 (Wind Electric Power Generation).
- List companies in NAICS 441110 (New Car Dealers) in Washington State's King County.
- List search firms that recruit executives for NAICS 3254 (Pharmaceutical & Medicine Manufacturing).
- List venture capital firms that invest in AI startups (NAICS 541745).
- List private equity firms that acquire turnaround clothing retailers (NAICS 448110).

With each of these prompts, you're not guessing about what jobs are available, you're instructing AI to mine an existing system that classifies the entire economy.

BEAT GHOST JOBS AND GENERIC POSTINGS WITH NAICS SEARCHES

As discussed in Chapter 11, when you've been labeled as too good to hire, one of the worst mistakes you can make is narrowing your search to what's visible online. Ghost jobs and generic postings don't represent the real market. NAICS codes give you a structured way to break out of that trap.

Instead of saying, "I guess I'll apply to this operations role at H&M and hope for the best," you're now saying, "I know the exact industry H&M belongs to. I know every competitor. I can find who's hiring in my city, in my function, or in adjacent subsectors."

Understanding how to leverage NAICS codes to find available jobs changes the game from hoping you're considered for a role to knowing you've applied to a real, available position within a company.

With NAICS codes, you don't need to limit yourself to posted jobs or companies that happen to be top of mind. Now, every time you think of a company you'd like to work for, pull its NAICS code, and multiply that bit of data into a list of ten, twenty, or fifty more related companies using AI to do the research for you. That's how you build leverage. That's how you stop feeling boxed in. And that's how you find your way back into a job market that desperately needs your experience — whether it realizes it yet or not.

CHAPTER 13

THE HALF-PAGE HANDSHAKE: WRITING A COVER LETTER THAT GETS READ

Two days later, Elaine slid her laptop across the table toward me. We were back at the coffee shop for another meeting. "Here's my latest cover letter," she said.

I scanned the four long paragraphs, stiff language, and generic phrases. "Elaine," I said, "this sounds like a Wikipedia page. No one is reading this."

She sighed. "But every template online says to cover my background in detail."

"Those templates are built for the lowest common denominator. You're overqualified, which means you need to write like a human. Think of your cover letter as a half-page handshake. The goal isn't to dump your career history onto the page, it's to make the reader like you enough to open your resume."

After a bit of work, we cut Elaine's cover letter down to three short paragraphs that included an opener showing she knew the company's current priorities, a middle tying her most relevant experience to those priorities, and a closing line that made her sound approachable, not desperate.

"With this three-paragraph approach, you're telling them you get what they need and you're ready to help," I said.

COVER LETTERS ARE CONVERSATION STARTERS, NOT FORMAL GREETINGS

Daniel watched quietly as Elaine and I worked on rewriting her cover letter, then asked, "What about me?"

"The same rules apply to all cover letters," I said. "Brevity, relevance, warmth. A good cover letter is an invitation to a conversation, not a dissertation."

They both nodded, finally seeing that in a world where attention is short, a half-page can open more doors than a full one.

Interestingly, because companies now use resume scanning software, ATS filters, and high-volume applications, most job candidates skip cover letters entirely. And while it's true that cover letters are no longer read the way they used to be, if they're read at all, choosing to forgo a cover letter is a mistake — especially for you.

When you're seen as overqualified, your resume can trigger fears before it builds confidence. A great cover letter resets that narrative because it gives you a chance to speak directly to the hiring team as a person, not just a record of past achievements. Your cover letter is your first handshake with the hiring manager. And like a good handshake, it should be firm, short, and full of intent.

> **Your cover letter is your first handshake with the hiring manager. And like a good handshake, it should be firm, short, and full of intent.**

Where so many job seekers fail is when they submit a cover letter that's formatted like a corporate memo and sounds like it was written by a compliance officer. The result is a wall of jargon and self-congratulation that no one wants to read. Take a look at the following two sample cover letters which clearly show the difference between a dry, formal essay and a concise, inviting introduction.

The *Before* Cover Letter

Elaine D. Bransford
Richmond, Virginia 23226
elaine.bransford@email.com
(555) 555-3819

Hiring Committee
Google Cloud
Mountain View, California 94043

Dear Esteemed Members of the Hiring Committee,

It is with genuine enthusiasm and professional conviction that I submit this letter in formal application for the position of Partner Development Manager (PDM) at Google Cloud. I have long admired the organization's bold, innovative approach to cloud technology and its unwavering commitment to empowering enterprises through scalable, secure, and transformative solutions. I believe my decades of experience and academic grounding uniquely position me to contribute meaningfully to your continued success.

With more than 20 years of experience in the technology and consulting sectors, including more than a decade focused specifically on channel partnerships and enterprise-level cloud transformation, I bring a robust combination of strategic leadership and practical expertise. Throughout my career, I have held roles in business development, channel management, and technology integration, always with a view toward forging resilient partnerships that yield long-term value.

My educational background includes a master's degree in organizational strategy, with a research focus on the intersection of digital transformation and business resilience. This academic perspective has underpinned my ability to craft partner engagement strategies that not only drive revenue but also align with broader market shifts in cloud computing, consumption-based pricing models, and infrastructure scalability.

During my tenure in senior development roles at several US-based technology consultancies, I worked closely with software vendors, system integrators, and managed service providers to design and implement growth-oriented partnership plans. This included developing joint go-to-market strategies, overseeing sales enablement programs, and managing performance metrics for cloud adoption across multiple sectors, including healthcare, education, and public services.

I am particularly drawn to the PDM role at Google Cloud due to its emphasis on joint solution development, technical depth, and co-promotion of partner capabilities. I have consistently excelled at navigating the complexities of cloud ecosystem relationships, and I take great pride in my ability to distill highly technical offerings into compelling business narratives for both executive stakeholders and frontline sales teams.

My professional style is one of thoughtful persistence. I approach challenges with analytical rigor and seek to build bridges across functions, departments, and organizations. I am also known for my ability to translate strategic objectives into tactical execution, whether it involves leading a cross-functional partner initiative or guiding executive leadership through cloud economics and operational ROI.

In closing, I would be honored to bring my experience, insights, and enthusiasm to Google Cloud as a Partner Development Manager. I am excited by the opportunity to contribute to a team that is not only shaping the future of cloud computing but also doing so with integrity and foresight. I thank you for considering my application and would welcome the opportunity to speak further about how I might support your goals.

With sincere appreciation,
Elaine D. Bransford

The *After* Cover Letter

Elaine Bransford
Richmond, VA
elaine.bransford@email.com
(555) 555-3819

Dear Janet Austen and Google Cloud Hiring Team,

I want this role. Not just because I meet every qualification you've outlined, but because I have the potential to thrive in exactly this kind of environment — one built on team alignment, partnerships, and meaningful impact. After connecting with Jason Darcy and learning more about the team's direction, I knew I had to apply. I can see myself at Google Cloud for the rest of my career, and I don't say that lightly.

What draws me to your company is your mission to help organizations build what's next. That sense of collaborative solutions-first thinking isn't just exciting, it's how I've worked for years. I'm ready to be involved in partnerships with your system integrators, work cross-functionally with your team to scale cloud adoption strategies across verticals, and help clients modernize infrastructure by following your company processes. I understand what you need in this role: someone who can earn trust quickly, translate technical complexity into business value, and fit into your company's culture and do things your way. I can do that from day one.

I'm ready to bring energy, collaboration, and long-term commitment to your team. Let's talk about what comes next.

Warmly,
Elaine Bransford

KEEP YOUR COVER LETTER CONCISE AND FULL OF POTENTIAL

A great cover letter should fit on half a page. Ideally, it should be three short paragraphs.

1. The first paragraph should immediately communicate interest and long-term intent. Say clearly: "I want this job, and I see myself here for years."
2. The second paragraph should tie your background to what the company needs. This is where you show understanding of their goals and how you're built to contribute to them.
3. The third paragraph is a call to connection. You're not pitching anymore; you're opening the door. Let them feel how easy it would be to talk to you, how aligned you are with their mission, and how ready you are to move forward.

The after version of Elaine's cover letter works so well because it actually sounds like her. It expresses commitment, shows an understanding of the company's values, and puts her experience into context. She doesn't bury the lede, she starts strong by saying, "I want this role." And by ending the letter with "Let's talk about what comes next," she's politely giving the reader clear next steps. This is how you stand out when you're seen as having too much experience. You bring it to a human level. You use your cover letter to say, "I belong here. I've done the work. I'm ready to do more."

And this half-page handshake strategy is directly related to the work you did in Chapter 12. If you've already identified the companies and sectors that are right for you, then your cover letter isn't just a generic attachment; it's a bridge. It's the first moment of alignment between you and your ideal employer. When done right, your cover letter says what your resume never could: "I'm not just capable. I'm committed. And I'm choosing *you*."

Never skip the chance to say that. Never forfeit the handshake. Because when you're seen as overqualified, the most important thing you can be is *human*.

CHAPTER 14

SAY WHY OR SAY GOODBYE: OVERCOMING OBJECTIONS IN YOUR COVER LETTER

Daniel's cover letter draft started with, "I'm applying for the position of..."

I stopped reading right there and said, "Daniel, if they've opened your cover letter, they already know what role you're applying for. You've wasted your first line."

He looked frustrated. "Then what do I start with?" he asked.

"You start by saying *why them*. As in, why do you want to be a part of their organization, specifically? Why are they special to you? If you don't do that, you're just another generic applicant and they'll move on to the next person in the pile."

Daniel's expression made it clear he hadn't totally bought into what I was saying, so I added, "One time I had a client who opened her cover letter with a single line referencing the company's recent acquisition and how her skills could help integrate the two businesses. She got the interview because she showed she was paying attention."

Daniel admitted he'd never mentioned why he wanted to work for the company in any of his applications. "I figured the resume spoke for itself," he said.

I shook my head. "It doesn't. Overqualified candidates are assumed to be applying to dozens of jobs. If you don't tell them why this one matters to you, they assume it doesn't."

As we worked, I said, "If you can't tell them why, you might as well not apply. Because if they can't see your genuine interest, you're just another resume in the pile."

START (AND END) WITH WHY

If you're seen as overqualified, the hiring manager already has questions about your intent. Why would someone with your level of experience want this job? Are you really committed, or just passing time until something better comes along? Are you going to demand too much money? Are you trying to downshift into an easy role before retirement? Or will you grow frustrated and leave the moment you're challenged?

From your perspective, these questions might sound absurd, but I assure you, they're standard, predictable concerns that follow highly capable candidates. And the only way to disarm them is to address them directly in your cover letter before they ever become a reason to reject you.

Always remember, hiring is a risk. And when a candidate appears too good, the risk feels bigger, not smaller. It doesn't matter if your resume is flawless. It doesn't matter if your interviews go well. If the hiring manager can't figure out why you want the role, they'll pass.

That's why your cover letter needs to tell the hiring manager why you've chosen their company before they can even ask, "Why this company? Why this role? Why now?" If you don't, they'll make up a reason that works for *them*, and it usually ends in a rejection email. As a high-capability candidate, this is your opportunity to set the tone and reframe the narrative.

HANDLE OBJECTIONS BEFORE A HIRING MANAGER CAN THINK THEM

As an overqualified job candidate, you will face more objections than young, underqualified candidates. Employers may think you'll ask for too much money. That you'll leave for a better job soon. That you'll be too rigid to adapt to their team. That you're near retirement and not invested. That you'll make others feel threatened. Or that you're hiding a red flag, like being fired from a previous role. These are real concerns. But they're not insurmountable if you meet them head-on with clarity and intent.

If you're worried about being seen as a short-term hire, say so. Try language like: "I'm looking for a long-term home, not just a job. I plan to work for the next 15-20 years, and I want that time to be spent building something meaningful with your team." That kind of directness tells them you've thought it through.

If you sense they may assume you're too expensive, say: "While I bring years of experience, I'm not driven by title or compensation. I'm motivated by doing work that matters, and this role is the right fit for what I want to contribute next."

If they might question your motivation altogether, explain: "I've followed your company's mission for years, and working here has always been a career goal for me. This isn't a fallback. It's a fit."

The goal is to *close the loop* with your cover letter. Don't just hope the hiring manager interprets your application correctly. Guide their perception of you from the start. Use your cover letter to show that your intentions are sincere, your expectations are realistic, and your commitment is real. Let them see that you didn't stumble onto their job posting. You chose it, and more importantly, *them*.

> **The goal is to *close the loop* with your cover letter. Don't just hope the hiring manager interprets your application correctly. Guide their perception of you from the start.**

DROP THE CORPORATE TONE AND NEVER USE AI SLOP

It's tempting to let AI write your cover letter for you, but I encourage you to take a stab at writing it yourself. You need to be human in your cover letter and use real language to say what you actually mean in your own voice.

When you say things like, "I want to grow with a company that shares my values," or, "I'm ready to focus on impact, not just advancement," or, "This role matches where I am now and where I want to be," objections dissolve. Infusing your personality professionally and concisely into your cover letter let's a hiring manager know they're hiring a real person who sees them clearly, who knows what they want, and who has already taken the first step toward belonging.

In today's corporate landscape, a cover letter isn't a space to brag or summarize your resume. It's an opportunity for you to highlight why you want the job, why you're a match, and why you've chosen them. If you don't say it like you mean it, you're giving them permission to say goodbye.

CHAPTER 15

A LINE OF ACCOUNTABILITY: ADD TWO NAMES TO YOUR COVER LETTER

After talking to Daniel, I turned back to Elaine. She handed me another cover letter draft — this one starting with "Dear Hiring Manager."

I pushed it back across the table and said, "Elaine, that's the cover letter equivalent of saying, 'To Whom It May Concern.'"

She frowned. "But sometimes I can't find a name."

"Then you're not looking hard enough," I said.

I showed her how to find a likely hiring manager on LinkedIn by searching for the job title plus the company name, or by filtering for people in the department. Even if the exact person wasn't clear, finding someone senior in that function was better than a generic greeting.

Daniel leaned in. "What if I get it wrong?"

"Then you still look more engaged than ninety percent of candidates. No one penalizes effort in this situation — they penalize apathy. Today, addressing someone by name shows initiative."

"When someone sees their own name at the top of a cover letter," I said, "they feel a sense of connection before they even read the first sentence. That's the first crack in the wall between stranger and hire."

IF YOU CAN'T BE TROUBLED TO FIND THEIR NAME, THEY CAN'T BE TROUBLED TO INTERVIEW YOU

Generic greetings are the first red flag in a cover letter that will land your application in the pass pile. When a hiring manager sees "To Whom It May Concern" or "Dear Hiring Committee," they know you didn't care enough to find out who's behind the role. And if you didn't care enough to do that, what else didn't you care enough to do?

You don't need to know the exact name of the person hiring, but you do need to find someone *close* enough to the decision to show that you looked. That one small step signals initiative. It signals respect. And it radically increases your chances of getting a reply.

Today, anyone can search the employees of any company using LinkedIn's free tools. You don't need a premium account. Just go to the company's LinkedIn page, click on "People," and start narrowing down the options. If the company is large, over 1,000 employees, your best bet is to look for someone in talent acquisition, internal recruiting, or HR.

Use search terms like "talent acquisition specialist," "technical recruiter," "corporate recruiter," or "people operations." If the company is smaller, under 1,000 people, shift your focus to potential hiring managers. This means searching for the department heads or team leads of the role you're applying to. For very small companies under 100 employees, operations managers, directors, or even the CEO may be the person responsible for hiring.

Once you've identified someone reasonably close to the role of the hiring manager, you can address your cover letter directly to them, followed by "and team." This strategy gives you a name to reference while also covering the possibility that someone else will review your materials.

For example: "Dear Jane Doe and team." If Jane isn't the right person, she'll forward your email to the one who is, especially if she sits in the same office. That's the logic behind adding the location filter to your LinkedIn search. By narrowing employees down to the local office responsible for the role, you turn a company of 150,000 into a shortlist of 12. Now Jane Doe isn't just someone random. She's one of a few likely candidates for hiring authority, or knows who is.

AFTER YOU FIND A GATEKEEPER, FIND A PROXIMAL CONTACT

There's another layer to this strategy. You can, and should, mention a relevant employee in the body of your cover letter. This doesn't require a full referral or a long exchange. Just referencing a person at the company with a similar job title or within the same department raises the stakes. This person is known as a *proximal contact.*

You can find a proximal contact by using the same LinkedIn employee search method but replacing talent acquisition keywords with the actual job title you're applying to, e.g., "project manager," "UX designer," "product analyst." Add the same location filter. Then connect with several of these people. Even if they don't respond right away, you can still reference the connection in your cover letter. Say something simple and true: "I recently connected with John Smith on LinkedIn, and shortly after, discovered this opening, which I believe I'm a strong match for."

That single sentence will change how the hiring manager views your application. Why? Because they don't know the nature of your connection. They don't know if you had a call, exchanged emails, or if John Smith plans to follow up with them about you tomorrow. All they know is that someone inside the company is linked to you, and that makes ignoring your application riskier. The higher the visibility you have within their network, the less comfortable they'll feel rejecting you without cause. Even if your experience isn't a perfect match, they're more likely to take a second look because you've created a line of accountability.

NAME-DROPPING ADDS POSITIVE PRESSURE

Too many job seekers still think that spending time to find the name of the hiring manager or someone closely related is optional. They think addressing a letter to a real person is only necessary if that person is listed in the job description. But as we've covered in earlier chapters, one of the primary things that gives your application weight is *relevance*, and nothing is more relevant than showing you've already made contact with the team.

A good handshake doesn't go to a committee; it goes to a person. If you want to stand out and be taken seriously, you need to start your cover letter like you started your job search: by focusing on people, not just postings.

CHAPTER 16

THE TWO REAL RESUME FORMATS THAT MATTER TODAY

The next day, Daniel brought me a resume that looked like it had been pulled straight from 1999 — dense text, Times New Roman, no white space. Elaine's was the opposite — overdesigned, multiple columns, fancy fonts. Both would fail for different reasons.

"There are only two resume formats that you need to consider as a highly qualified candidate: chronological and functional. Chronological works if you've been steadily employed and your job titles line up with the one you want now," I explained. "Functional works for almost everyone else, especially if you're overqualified or have career gaps, because it lets you lead with skills and results instead of just dates."

Elaine perked up. "So, I can move my achievements to the top?"

"Exactly. You want to control the narrative. The AI system employers are using to pre-scan applications doesn't care if your resume looks pretty; it cares if it's scannable, keyword-rich, and in the right format. The humans who see it after that care about a clean, logical flow."

Daniel nodded slowly. "So, it's less about impressing and more about removing friction?"

"Exactly," I said. "Think of your resume as a pass-through device. Its only job is to survive the AI filter and give a human no reason to throw it out in the first ten seconds."

THE TWO RESUME FORMATS THAT ACTUALLY WORK

Every job platform, resume builder, and so-called career expert over the past 30 years has tried to sell the idea that there are thousands of ways to format a resume. That if you just find the *right* design, if you pick the perfect font or the trendiest color scheme, if you choose between boxes, arrows, icons, or columns, you'll finally land the job. But that's marketing, not truth.

There are really only two resume formats that matter: chronological and functional. Everything else is a variation on these two foundations.

> There are really only two resume formats that matter: chronological and functional. Everything else is a variation on these two foundations.

The Chronological Resume

Chronological resumes are what most people are familiar with. They list jobs in reverse date order, beginning with your most recent title and working backward. They work well when you have experience in the field you're applying to and when that experience lines up cleanly with the job title you want next.

If you're progressing in a career linearly, like going from project manager to senior project manager, this resume format helps reinforce that. It's especially effective when the person reading your resume is a human who can interpret patterns, make assumptions, and give you the benefit of the doubt. Chronological resumes can also work well when you're applying directly to a company you've already had some interaction with, or if you're being referred internally by someone who can explain your background.

But what happens when the person reviewing your resume isn't a person at all?

Thanks to AI resume filters and profile analysis tools, chronological resumes are now a liability in many job searches. If you haven't held the exact job title the employer is looking for, you can be screened out. If you have a gap on your resume, even for valid reasons like caregiving, illness, or a sabbatical, you can be excluded. If your experience is too old, or the date ranges too long, you can get filtered out for being "too senior" or "outdated." If you're trying to switch industries or re-enter the workforce after time away, the chronological format highlights your differences, not your fit. This is why overqualified job candidates in particular must be cautious. A chronological format tends to shine a light on your age, career shifts, and past roles that may confuse AI filters and recruiters alike. And confusion leads to rejection.

The Functional Resume

A functional resume organizes your qualifications by relevance, not chronology. Instead of presenting your jobs as a timeline, you present your capabilities grouped by the skills and experience most aligned to the job you want. This is why the functional resume format becomes not just helpful, but necessary.

With this format, you lead with functions, not dates. Instead of opening your work history with, "Senior Vice President, Company Has A Name, 2014–2019," you open with something like, "Executive Leadership Experience," followed by bullet points describing leadership activities you've performed, regardless of where or when you did them. Only after showcasing your most job-relevant skills do you list the roles and organizations where those skills were gained. You put the spotlight on what you *can do*, not on what your title *was*.

This structure is particularly useful for anyone who:

- Doesn't have the exact job title in their work history.
- Has held multiple roles that don't obviously align with the one they're applying for.
- Took a career break, whether for caregiving, illness, entrepreneurship, or retirement.
- Is switching industries or job functions altogether.
- Is older or seen as overqualified, and needs to control the narrative before age-based assumptions kick in.

The functional resume allows you to take control of your story and organize your value in a way that AI filters can recognize.

DON'T MAKE EMPLOYERS CONNECT THE DOTS IN YOUR RESUME

As the Wall Street Journal reports, recruiters today still spend an average of only six seconds scanning a resume before deciding whether to pass or proceed. That's not enough time to decipher your past. It's enough time to match what's in front of them to what's in their job description. If you don't make that match fast and obvious, you're out.[14]

Functional resumes make that match. Instead of forcing a recruiter or algorithm to connect the dots, a functional resume draws the picture for them. You include your keywords up front and then the job title, skills, and the context behind them. For example:

Senior Program Management Skills
Gained as Senior Operations Manager at Intel and as Program Lead at Kellogg

- Ready to collaborate cross-functionally as demonstrated by leading a 6-person team that secured $1.8M in funding by drafting competitive federal and private sector proposals.
- Positioned to manage a regulatory compliance team as evidenced by overhauling compliance SOPs to reduce audit findings to zero across 3 consecutive inspections.

THE TWO REAL RESUME FORMATS THAT MATTER TODAY

- Ability to set up new business development deals as shown by successfully negotiating more than 40 vendor contracts and supporting a national product launch on schedule.

It's clear, scannable, keyword-rich, and removes doubt. We will cover keywords more in Chapter 19.

Of course, many people, including outdated career coaches and HR bloggers, still resist the functional format.

Why? Because it demands more thought and customization. Because it's not what they're used to. Because they think it hides information. But in reality, it does the opposite; it *reveals* what's relevant and it *removes* distractions. It also helps restore clarity to job seekers with nontraditional or high-capability backgrounds.

WHICH RESUME FORMAT SHOULD YOU CHOOSE?

If you're applying for a job you've done before, in a field you've stayed in, and your titles match up exactly, use a chronological resume. But if your career has twists, pivots, or long stretches that don't obviously align with the role you want, use a functional resume. If your dates could work against you, or if your story is stronger when it's told in terms of what you *offer* rather than what you *did*, go functional.

Everything else — designer formats, infographic layouts, colorful templates — is just window dressing. Don't buy into gimmicks. You don't need trendy. You need clarity. You need matchability. You need to control how your experience is read. And in many cases, that means putting relevance first and dates second.

In the next chapter, we'll look at how these formats are now converging into a single powerful format: the hybrid resume.

CHAPTER 17

THE HYBRID RESUME: THE NEW STANDARD FOR OVERQUALIFIED JOB SEEKERS

Elaine's eyes lit up when I showed her the hybrid resume format later that day. "This makes so much more sense for me," she said.

The top third featured a professional summary followed by a work experience section that grouped relevant experiences together functionally, but also in reverse chronological order using broad date ranges.

Daniel resisted at first. "It feels like I'm hiding something," he said.

"You're not hiding, you're framing," I told him. "The old format works against you because it leads with your age, seniority, and length of career. The hybrid format lets you lead with relevance."

Wanting to remind them of what we'd discussed during our first meeting, I said, "Once people label you, it's hard to get unlabeled. A resume that starts with '35 years of experience' instantly screams, 'expensive and overqualified' to the wrong eyes."

With the hybrid resume format now in play, we rebuilt their resumes line by line, ensuring the skills section mirrored the job posting and the achievements showed measurable results. "Your resume should feel like it's been built for one job only," I said. "Because if it looks like you're applying to every job, it won't get picked for any."

THE HYBRID RESUME BUILDS A BRIDGE FOR THE EMPLOYER

If the chronological resume is a backward-looking document built on linear storytelling, and the functional resume is a forward-facing marketing tool designed to showcase relevance over time, then the hybrid resume is the bridge between both worlds. For overqualified job candidates — those who are deeply experienced, too educated, or both — and perhaps perceived as too advanced for many roles, the hybrid resume is essential.

> If the chronological resume is a backward-looking document built on linear storytelling, and the functional resume is a forward-facing marketing tool designed to showcase relevance over time, then the hybrid resume is the bridge between both worlds.

The hybrid format recognizes your achievements while allowing you to strategically control your narrative, hiding what hurts you and highlighting what gets you interviews. In a job market increasingly governed by keyword-matching AI filters and distracted hiring managers, the hybrid resume gives you both algorithmic visibility and human resonance.

Unlike a traditional chronological resume that forces you to present a career history in exact reverse order with hard dates, a hybrid resume allows you to group your experience by skill sets or functions, just like a functional resume, while still including date ranges and company names in a more flexible, blended way.

This format eliminates the most common liabilities for overqualified candidates: long gaps, outdated job titles, and overly technical or obscure career paths. At the same time, it doesn't omit dates entirely, which can raise red flags with some employers or systems that automatically downgrade resumes missing timeframes.

EXAMPLE HYBRID RESUME AND HOW TO CREATE ONE

Take a look at this example of Daniel's hybrid resume. Rather than squeezing his career into a single chronological line, it organizes his experiences into themed sections. These section titles act as narrative frames, signaling to both AI filters and human readers that he's not just summarizing job titles, but curating a story of transferable value.

Daniel Roberts, MBA

555.555.5574
danielroberts@email.com
www.linkedin.com/in/danielroberts555-555

Summary

Visionary and results-oriented leader with the ability to drive client success, team-centric initiatives and operational excellence. Ready to develop and execute comprehensive onboarding strategies, foster collaboration across cross-functional teams, and integrate new technologies to optimize client experiences following company protocols. Passionate about creating exceptional client experiences that align with the company's established strategic growth initiatives.

Work Experience

Vice President-Level Expertise & Client Success Onboarding Skills
2020-Present
Gained as Vice President, Client Services, Corporate, Inc., Assistant Vice President, Green Company and Head of Business and Market Development, Mass Strategy Co.

- Poised to contribute to cross-functional initiatives with increased autonomy and strategic foresight, building on a foundation of collaborative work across departments, as previously demonstrated by aligning contract terms across finance, IT, and supply chain, reducing negotiation cycles by 35%.
- Positioned to own high-stakes negotiations in emerging markets and technologies by expanding on complex commercial contracting skills, as shown by successfully managing and closing 50+ vendor and licensing agreements valued at over $60M in one year.
- Developing into a trusted adviser for growth-stage and global teams, with the agility to support high-speed decision-making, as evidenced by guiding international market entry decisions at Company Green, reducing regulatory risk exposure by 70% during early exploration.

Transformational Strategy, Client Engagement & Client Services Skills
2012-2020
Gained as Senior Vice President/Partner, Elevated Corporation Name, Gained as Vice President, Client Services, Corporate, Inc., Assistant Vice President, Green Company and Head of Business and Market Development, Mass Strategy Co.

- Equipped to translate insight from leadership into operational execution at scale and deliver timely

solutions, as previously demonstrated by accelerating contract review timelines by 60% across multiple business units during a rapid growth phase.
- Ready to help drive regulatory alignment in fast-evolving industries like renewables and energy infrastructure, as demonstrated by creating a compliance roadmap for an energy firm targeting US expansion, saving $2M in potential misaligned expenses.
- Set to be a part of cross-border strategy and localization with rising influence, drawing on early experience in international contracting, as shown by managing dispute resolutions and localizing more than 20 complex contracts across business sectors with zero increase in expenses.

Business Development & Market Development Expertise 2000-2012
Gained as Assistant Vice President, Green Company and Head of Business and Market Development, Mass Strategy Co.

- On track to elevate internal compliance systems through innovation and scalable frameworks, as previously demonstrated by launching a risk management training series that increased contract compliance rates by 42% within two quarters.
- Positioned to scale global communications and collaborate with distributed teams with clarity and impact, as shown by orchestrating multi-party alignment between business partners on warranty matters, resolving issues 3x faster than baseline timelines.
- Growing capacity to architect solutions for novel projects and evolving markets, as evidenced by developing and vetting new regulatory models for sustainable infrastructure that informed go/no-go decisions, saving $1.5M in sunk costs.

Education

- Master of Business Administration in Management & Marketing | Western Location University, City Name, CT
- Bachelor of Arts in Economics and Regulatory Affairs | State University, City Name, NY

Skills

- Client Success and Onboarding Excellence
- Employee Benefits Strategy
- Cross-Functional Collaboration
- Technology Integration and Data Optimization
- Strategic Growth and Market Development
- Lean Methodologies and Continuous Improvement
- Governance and Board Development
- Vendor Management and SLA Achievement
- Operational Leadership and Efficiency
- Communication and Stakeholder Engagement

Affiliations & Achievements

- Board of Directors, National Endowment for Important Cause
- Volunteer & Speaker, National Organization of Priority Initiatives
- Partner of the Year, AAAA and BBBB organizations
- Leadership Award, Organization Name
- Member, Society of Leadership Organization Member, Alliance of Collaborative Organization

Hobbies

- Horseback riding, water polo, camping

Daniel's bullet points strike a careful balance between possibility and proof. Future-oriented phrasing like "Poised to contribute to cross-functional initiatives" and "Equipped to translate insight from leadership into operational execution" convey readiness to collaborate and follow direction, while specifics such as "reducing negotiation cycles by 35%" and "saving $2M in potential misaligned expenses" prove he's already done it. As a result, and as thoroughly laid out with examples in Chapters 6 and 7, each of the resume's work experience section bullet points lead with potential and follows with proof that includes a quantified result. Collectively, the language used in Daniel's bullet points indicates high levels of agreeableness, as discussed in Chapters 8 and 9, showing that he both prioritizes working with others and doing things the company's way, not his way.

Daniel also avoids formatting traps that an AI system would flag as "too experienced" or that would signal he was "too senior" to a risk-averse hiring manager. There's no column of stacked dates on the left. Instead, dates are contextualized within descriptions, deflecting age bias while maintaining credibility. Daniel's keywords are specific and match the job description for this role with terms like "collaborate with distributed teams," "optimize client experiences," and "growth-stage and global teams," which dominate the page and are precisely the kind of phrasing AI systems prioritize.

This resume is machine-optimized and human-centered. Daniel doesn't come off as someone desperate for any role. He appears as someone ready to excel in a specific one. His hybrid format gives him total control over the first impression he makes, regardless of how his experience might have once been misread.

STOP WRITING YOUR OBITUARY AND START MARKETING YOURSELF

If you've been told you're too experienced, too educated, or not quite the right fit, chances are the problem is not your qualifications but how your qualifications are being perceived. A hybrid resume allows you to reframe your story and market yourself on your terms. It allows you to lead with relevance and strategic framing instead of a rigid timeline that penalizes you for doing too much, learning too widely, or taking time away from the workforce. This format is especially powerful for those returning from retirement, transitioning sectors, or navigating long gaps due to caregiving, health issues, or personal ventures.

To write a hybrid resume, start by identifying the top two to four functional skill sets you want to be hired for and that appear repeatedly in the job descriptions you're targeting. These will become your major sections. Under each section, list specific experiences that support those skill sets. Then, cite the company and role where each experience was gained, without grouping them chronologically. If a function spans many years, you can summarize the date range more generally, as seen in Daniel's resume example — Transformational Strategy, Client Engagement & Client Services Skills | 2012 - 2020 — without letting specific dates and gaps dominate the layout.

The hybrid resume format is an evolution necessary for finding success in today's market. In a hiring landscape where resumes are filtered in seconds and perception outweighs potential, this format positions you as the best of both worlds: someone who's done it all and is ready to do it again, with clarity, humility, and strategic alignment.

CHAPTER 18

THE SIX-PART RESUME STRUCTURE EMPLOYERS LOVE

Elaine had nine different sections on her resume, including professional affiliations, hobbies, publications, and even a philosophy section. Daniel had none labeled properly. I was determined to stay on the topic of resumes with them for as many days as it took to change their perspectives on what employers and their AI systems wanted to see.

That's when I told them, "You only need six sections in your resume: contact info, professional summary, professional experience, education, skills, and affiliations, awards, and hobbies. Everything else either belongs on LinkedIn or comes up in an interview."

Daniel asked, "But won't cutting things make me look less impressive?"

"No," I said. "It makes you look more relevant. Too much detail is like talking too much in an interview — you bury the good stuff."

I explained how each section had a purpose: contact info so they can reach you, summary so they want to, skills for keyword matching, experience for potential and proof, education for validation, and affiliations, awards and hobbies to humanize you. "Think of your resume as prime real estate," I said. "Every inch has to earn rent."

Elaine deleted three sections in under a minute. "Feels cleaner already," she said

If you're overqualified, there's a good chance your resume has already been overloaded, too many dates, too many roles, too much information crammed into too little space.

You've spent years, maybe decades, building up your expertise. You've earned awards, added degrees, taken leadership roles, and likely dabbled in several sectors. But when it comes to your resume, the key isn't to include everything you've ever done; it's to organize your career into six essential sections that every resume, no matter how advanced, must have. These six sections are:

1. Contact Information
2. Professional Summary
3. Work Experience
4. Education
5. Skills
6. Affiliations, Awards, Hobbies.

That's it. Everything else is clutter.

START WITH YOUR CONTACT INFORMATION AND A PROFESSIONAL SUMMARY

Start with the Contact Information section. This should be extremely lean. Name. Phone number. Professional email. LinkedIn URL. No address. Not your city. Not even your state. Including a location, even if you live down the street from the office, can create a perception problem. You might live on the "wrong" side of the city. Or, if the company is remote-first, they may assume you're not flexible. Worst of all, hiring managers might draw conclusions based on your zip code. Let your experience speak, not your geography.

Include your LinkedIn URL because today, hiring managers want to see a face. They want to check your digital presence. But never include a photo on your resume, at least not in the US, because of compliance issues. Let LinkedIn be your visual handshake. If you're in a field like writing, data science, UX, or any job where you can showcase a body of work, include one additional link to a digital portfolio or GitHub account. This is becoming standard in modern hiring and gives hiring managers a richer, more interactive view of your capabilities.

Next is your professional summary. Ditch the outdated "objective statement" once and for all. Instead, use this top third of your resume, which is known in the industry as the *visual center*, to give the employer exactly what they're looking for. Eye-tracking studies spanning more than 10 years and originally featured on ABC News show employers spend up to 80% of their viewing time in this top section. That's why AI filters today heavily weight this area too.[15] You can use a brief paragraph or three strong bullet points here. This isn't the place to be vague. It's where you call out your target job title, your top two or three skills, and a clear value statement. If you don't do this, the employer won't bother reading on. Think of it as your elevator pitch in print.

WRITE A CONTROLLED WORK EXPERIENCE SECTION FOLLOWED BY YOUR EDUCATION

Then comes Work Experience, which should flow based on the resume format you're using. As discussed in earlier chapters, if you're using a chronological resume, this will list roles and companies in reverse order. If you're using a functional format, you'll group experiences by skill sets. And if you're using a hybrid format, the most powerful option for overqualified candidates, your first experience section should be titled after the job you want, not the job you had. Eye-tracking data proves that employers look at the very first role or skill group in this section next after the professional summary. That's where they decide whether to keep reading. Make it count.

Education follows. While the academic instinct may be to list every degree, you don't have to. If you have multiple degrees in the same discipline, list the most advanced one. You don't need to include your bachelor's if it mirrors your master's or beyond such as a doctorate. You also don't need to include your GPA or graduation year. Keep this section focused on credentials that add dimension or show breadth.

END THE RESUME WITH A SKILLS, AFFILIATIONS, AND ACHIEVEMENTS

The Skills section is more strategic than ever. This isn't fluff. It's a keyword match exercise designed to beat AI filters. Choose 8–12 key skills listed in the job description, technical, transferable, or otherwise, and place them in a single column, left-justified. Avoid fancy formatting or multiple columns. Most AI systems today still struggle to parse resumes with complex layouts. Simple is smart. Group your skills naturally, software, certifications, methodologies, etc., but don't overthink it. Your goal is to mirror the language of the job description.

Finally, close with an Affiliations & Awards section that includes at least a few humanizing hobbies at the very end. This is where you drive home that you're someone who can thrive on a team. Include volunteer work, awards, affiliations, hobbies, and anything else that paints a picture of you as someone interesting and well-rounded. This isn't just filler. Hiring managers often mention this section during interviews because it's how they relate to you. "Oh, you love hiking? So do I." Suddenly, the conversation shifts from interview to connection. Include anything that reveals character, languages, certifications, public speaking, even media mentions.

These six sections are all you need. They serve the dual purpose of communicating competence and approachability. If you're overqualified, this is the structure that keeps your value in focus and your experience digestible. Don't add more. Don't overdesign. Don't try to impress by sheer volume. Let the framework do the work.

CHAPTER 19

THINK LIKE AI: KEYWORD DENSITY AND THE VISUAL CENTER

Daniel came to our next session holding three full pages with narrow margins, the space in between was crammed with every project he'd ever led. He dropped it on the table with a thud. "This is the one I've been sending out," he said proudly.

I opened my laptop and opened the electronic version he emailed me before arriving. I clicked to see the word count. "1,326 words," I said.

Daniel raised an eyebrow. "So what?" he asked.

"Most Applicant Tracking Systems reject anything over 700 words," I told him. "With a resume this long, you're invisible before they even read your name."

His face fell. "But I made so many cuts after our last session. If I cut even more, I'll look like I haven't done enough."

Elaine jumped in. "I used to think the same thing. Remember my old resume? Three columns, graphics, the whole thing? No one saw it. Once I stripped it back, I actually started getting calls."

Daniel looked unconvinced, so I gave him an example of a bullet point that was clear but impactful: Ready to take on strategic operations projects at Company X, leveraging proven results in project management, data analysis, and cross-functional collaboration.

"See what's happening here?" I asked. "Seven keywords in one bullet. Front-loaded. Under 20 words. This is how you get density without clutter."

I reminded them both that targeting wasn't about sounding impressive. It was about speaking directly to the machine before the human ever saw their resume. "You think cutting feels like losing," I told Daniel. "But trimming is how you win. Precision beats volume every time."

He sighed, then nodded slowly. "Alright. Show me how to cut it in half without losing the heart of it."

If there's one part of the job search process that drives even the most accomplished professionals to the brink, it's targeting a resume. You might go from never targeting your resume at all to spending hours tailoring it for a job you really want, only to get nothing in return. No interview. No follow-up. Not even an automated rejection. Just silence.

After a few rounds of this, most people give up, slipping back into using the same resume for every job until they finally burn out entirely. This chapter will keep you from ever reaching that point, because once you know how to target a resume the right way, it becomes a fast, 10 to 15-minute process.

IMPOSTER SYNDROME AND POSTURING ARE MAKING YOU INVISIBLE

The first thing to understand about writing an effective, targeted resume is that there are two major obstacles you must overcome: your own mind and the curse of knowledge. As a senior-level, educated professional, you're used to nuance. You assume the person evaluating your resume has the same depth of expertise you do. They don't.

In fact, the hiring manager is increasingly likely to be someone with an associate degree, or no degree at all, who was working in a completely different field less than a year ago. Seriously. Many Fortune 500 companies now fill recruiter roles with people who simply manage dashboards of AI hiring tools, replacing expensive senior HR professionals. Your resume must be written for that audience, and for the AI itself, not for a peer who understands your field.

The first thing to understand about writing an effective, targeted resume is that there are two major obstacles you must overcome: your own mind and the curse of knowledge.

Overqualified candidates often hesitate to put a keyword from a job posting on their resume unless they can get someone else's approval or an exact definition from the hiring manager. They think, *Well, I don't want to be unethical.* Or, *I need someone to define what they mean by this over the phone before I can say I did it or that I can do it.*

This hesitation is called impostor syndrome and it's a mistake that ruins careers. In reality, you don't need perfect agreement on what a term means, you just need it on your resume.

Take "digital transformation," for example. Many job seekers avoid using the phrase in their resume because it sounds technical or undefined, when really, it could mean something as simple as transferring survey results into a software system. Corporate jargon exists to make basic tasks sound impressive. Don't disqualify yourself from matching a keyword because you've overanalyzed it.

The second obstacle is posturing through your vocabulary habits. Habits that make you sound too distant and unrelatable to hiring managers. In professional writing, you've been trained to avoid repeating phrases because doing so feels sloppy. On resumes, repetition is essential. AI-driven Applicant Tracking Systems (ATS) measure keyword density, not literary elegance. If "project management" appears once on your resume, you're invisible. Most ATS today require a keyword density between 0.25% and 1% to mark your resume as targeted. Keyword density has been heavily used by the tech industry for ranking the credibility of everything from websites to scientific studies.[16] Now, they've come for your resume.

KEYWORD DENSITY PROTECTS EMPLOYERS AGAINST WHITE-FONT TRICKS

This new keyword density rule was developed in response to tricks like "white-fonting," where a job candidate includes the entire job posting at the end of their resume in 3-point, white font so their resume would be a fake, 100% match according to the AI scanners. Of course, this now registers its own red flag.

On a resume between 400 and 700 words — which is the range many systems now require to avoid gaming the system — you'd need to list project management at least twice to meet the targeting threshold. Less than that, and you won't even register as relevant.

This is why you must break free of the I-can't-repeat-myself mindset. Or, more practically, the I-have-to-use-a-thesaurus-to-come-up-with-a-different-word mindset. In resume targeting, redundancy is power.

It's also important to note that to successfully target your resume, you must also use exact matches to the language used in the job posting. No partial credit is given for variations in phrasing. If the posting says "cross-functional collaboration" with a dash, you must write it like that exactly in your resume. If it says "projects" instead of "project," match the plural. If the grammar in the posting is wrong, don't fix it; match it. ATS is not grading your English; it's matching patterns.

Also focus on long-tail keywords, specific multi-word phrases like "learning and development," "strategic operations," or "clinical research and development." These carry far more weight than short, generic words like "management" or "training." And don't forget to include the exact job title from the posting, even if it's long or includes a location. Place it in the first bullet of your summary and again in your experience section.

AI AND ATS SOFTWARE TOOLS ARE BOTH SMART AND DUMB

When it comes to formatting, remember that while AI-driven ATS tools have helped expedite the applicant review process, the software is still pretty dumb. Avoid shrinking margins to fit more text because anything outside a one-inch margin may be flagged as suspicious due to old, white-font, keyword-stuffing tricks. Don't upload a PDF unless the posting explicitly says so, as many systems flatten PDF text into an unreadable format. You should also leave out horizontal lines, complex columns, or graphics in the top section, since these can break parsing entirely.

Most importantly, front-load your keywords into the top third of the first page, where eye-tracking studies show hiring managers spend 80% of their time. And don't be afraid to stack multiple keywords into one bullet. For example:

- Ready to take on data-driven projects using agile project management methods, including projects requiring data analysis and cross-functional collaboration with a matrix team, previously achieving a 30% increase in project performance.

That single bullet contains six distinct keywords:

1. Data-driven projects
2. Agile project management methods
3. Data analysis
4. Cross-functional collaboration
5. Matrix team
6. Project performance

USE THE SKILLS SECTION TO BOOST KEYWORD DENSITY

Finally, use your skills section to repeat the exact same keywords you've already placed in your bullets. This doubles your count and helps you hit the density target. Your goal is to ensure every major keyword from the job posting appears at least twice, ideally once in your summary or experience and once in your skills list.

When you strip away the overthinking, resume targeting is less about sounding impressive and more about matching the job posting with precision, so the AI filter passes you to a human. Once you commit to that, and once you stop imagining that the reviewer is a more capable version of yourself, you'll cut your targeting time from hours to minutes, while dramatically increasing your odds of making it through the first round.

CHAPTER 20

MAKE THE MOST OF YOUR HONORS, HOBBIES, AND AWARDS SECTION

Not only was Daniel's resume dense; it also read like a eulogy. Elaine's was similar. It was as if they were documenting a life that had already happened, not pitching themselves for a life still to come.

"Your resume is not just your work history. It's not an obituary," I said. "It's a marketing piece. And like any good ad, it needs to sound human."

"When you strip all the life out of your resume, you disappear into the stack," I told them. "Machines filter you first, but humans hire you. Give them something that reminds them you're alive."

There's one part of the resume that job seekers, especially high-capability, overqualified candidates, often overlook or dismiss as fluff: the so-called "extracurricular" section.

Sometimes called Affiliations and Awards, Honors and Hobbies, Volunteer Work and Media Mentions, or Additional Activities, this small patch of text at the bottom of the page can determine whether your resume leaves a lasting impression or falls flat. In today's hiring market, it's your chance to humanize yourself — something that matters more than ever.

In fact, companies are investing heavily in AI systems designed to detect personality signals early, including on resumes and LinkedIn profiles. These systems are not only looking for specific keywords, but they're also scanning for tone, intent, and traits associated with strong workplace cohesion.

So, how does crafting a clear and strategic final section on your resume help you pass AI pre-selection and impress hiring managers?

AFFILIATIONS INCREASE YOUR AGREEABLENESS AND EXTRAVERSION SCORES

In a landmark study titled "Using Available Signals on LinkedIn for Personality Assessment," researchers analyzed the Big Five personality traits (go back and review Chapter 8 if you need a refresher) of more than 1,100 LinkedIn users using public profile content.[17]

The goal of the study was to determine whether profile data could predict personality, and by extension, job fit. What the researchers found was that *extracurriculars*, especially volunteer experiences, memberships, sports involvement, and certifications, are consistently tied to higher levels of Extraversion and Agreeableness.

Why does this matter? Because those two traits, Extraversion and Agreeableness, are among the most desired in today's team-based, remote-hybrid, turnover-sensitive work environments. Hiring managers want someone who shows signs of being energetic, sociable, kind, and cooperative. Someone who won't just perform, they'll build bridges, resolve tension, and attract other great hires. Those are glue people. And glue people reduce turnover. They're not a flight risk. They lift others. They stay.

And not only do Extraversion and Agreeableness signal high levels of likability, studies from organizations like EY and Deloitte have shown that people who play organized sports or belong to external organizations tend to outperform in leadership and team roles. It's not the soccer itself, it's the structure, communication, accountability, and humility that come with showing up for others outside of a paycheck.

So, while you may see that bottom section of your resume as optional, employers don't. It's your chance to hint at who you are off the clock. Are you part of a local running club or board game night? Do you volunteer at your kids' school? Did you earn a certification in design, creative writing, or data visualization in your free time? Have you contributed to open-source projects or written guest columns on industry blogs? Mention it. Not to show off. But to show up as a full person. To signal culture fit, likability, and longevity.

Most important of all, the AI systems employers are using now are scanning for exactly this kind of well-roundedness. If your resume or LinkedIn profile is stripped of personality, if it's just cold metrics and job titles, you're losing to candidates who show even a hint of Extraversion and Agreeableness. That's why in the next chapters, I'll show you how to re-engineer your digital presence to automatically reflect the traits employers are scanning for, before you even say a word.

But before reading on, revisit your resume, look at the final section, and ask yourself: *What does this say about the kind of teammate I'll be?* If the answer is "not much," then it's time to humanize your value.

SECTION THREE

YOU'RE BEING PROFILED AND SCORED BY EMPLOYERS

CHAPTER 21

YOUR RESUME AND LINKEDIN PROFILE ARE PERSONALITY TESTS

Three weeks into our work together, Elaine and Daniel joined me online in a virtual meeting to review their job search progress and talk about their wins and losses. Elaine's LinkedIn profile was not showing up in many search results, so I asked her what she'd done to improve her profile.

"I added a lot of keywords. Isn't that enough to make a difference?" she said with a frown.

"Not anymore," I replied. "AI filters, including LinkedIn's AI agents, aren't just looking at keywords; they're assessing personality markers. And the hiring managers who see it after that? They're looking for tone. It's the same AI-human process used for your resume but applied to your digital footprint."

I explained that even short bullet points reveal whether you're detail-oriented, big-picture focused, results-driven, agreeable, or rigid. Machines scan for patterns, like whether you emphasize collaboration, initiative, or authority.

Daniel leaned back. "So... they're profiling us before we even speak?"

"Yes. And if your resume and LinkedIn read like a cold technical manual, it signals low warmth, low adaptability. If they read like a vague self-help book, it signals fluff and no substance. The balance you need to strike combines results and approachability."

Daniel laughed bitterly. "It feels like a crime show."

"It's not personal," I said. "It's predictive analytics. Employers are building a profile based on everything you submit and everything they can find about you — especially on LinkedIn."

Elaine asked, "So we can't control it?"

"You can influence it," I said. "That's the game now. Consistency across resumes, LinkedIn, and public profiles matters. Even the words you use repeatedly become part of your digital signature."

We started improving their online profiles by auditing their LinkedIn profiles and resumes side by side, removing mismatched job titles and aligning their key phrases. "Every inconsistency is a red flag to a machine," I said. "And machines don't forget."

Reviewing their documents through that lens, Daniel added more collaborative language like *partnered*, *engaged*, and *aligned* to offset his authoritative tone. Elaine added more measurable results to ground her people-oriented narrative.

YOU CANNOT OPT OUT OF BEING PROFILED BY AI

Many overqualified candidates think they can opt out of AI scrutiny by simply staying offline and keeping things "professional." But in reality, AI is already in the application system. It's analyzing your word choice, the order of your bullet points, and the tone of your short answer about why you want the job. These systems are harvesting signals you don't even realize you're sending.

The latest research from Eric Grunenberg and colleagues, a premier social psychology and business research team with researchers spanning from the University of Münster in Germany to Columbia University Business School in New York, published in their *Frontiers in Social Psychology* article, "Machine learning in recruiting: predicting personality from CVs and short text responses," shows just how far this has come.[18] In one of the most illuminating studies to date, machine learning models were trained to predict the *entire Big Five* personality profile of job applicants, using nothing more than the resume and a brief written response about personal interests. No social media. No video interviews. Just the application itself.

The model's predictions, based *only* on the resume and a few sentences of text, correlated with actual personality scores at about r = 0.25 on average. This means the AI's guesses about someone's personality from their resume and short writing matched the person's actual personality test results about 25% of the way, which is considered a meaningful correlation in psychology.

In simple terms, the AI system could pick up on real personality traits just from how someone wrote about themselves. This is the same level of predictive accuracy seen in earlier studies using far richer sources like Facebook behavior or entire email histories. Even more telling, the AI outperformed human recruiters, who could only estimate Extraversion slightly above random chance.

And that's the point. These machines are better than people at reading between the lines. They're more consistent, less distracted, and they don't get bored. If your resume and application suggest that you're introverted, skeptical, negative, or too self-focused — whether you actually are or not —AI will catch it.

Worse, these traits are exactly what keep overqualified candidates stuck in limbo. You may be conscientious in real life, but do you come across as rigid on paper? You may be experienced, but do you sound controlling? You may be passionate, but do you sound reactive or scattered?

ALGORITHMS TREAT YOUR RESUME AND LINKEDIN PROFILE LIKE PSYCHOLOGICAL X-RAYS

A related study, which we referred to in the previous chapter, "Using Available Signals on LinkedIn for Personality Assessment," found that even minimal user behavior — likes, comments, short profile bios — was enough to generate strong predictions about Extraversion and Agreeableness. Remember, those are the two traits that consistently correlate with callback rates, interviews, and offers.

Interestingly, these two studies found that experience alone, especially when framed in isolation, signaled high Conscientiousness and low Agreeableness. That's the profile of someone who might perform well but also challenge the status quo. Someone who might ask for more and might not stick around. Two risks all employers see in overqualified job candidates.

These algorithms are *not just reading your resume* to see if you've had the job title before. They're reading it to assess whether you *sound like someone others would want to work with*. Employers want someone who will show up with enthusiasm, take feedback well, collaborate smoothly, and stick around long enough to matter. This is why listing "hardworking, detail-oriented, results-driven" on your resume and LinkedIn isn't enough.

AI can already tell how conscientious you are. What it's trying to figure out is: *Are you likable? Are you flexible? Are you someone we want on the team?*

In other words, your resume and LinkedIn profiles are now diagnostic tests. Everything you write, post, react to, or

> **Your resume and LinkedIn profiles are now diagnostic tests. Everything you write, post, react to, or send in a message is a data point used by AI to decide whether you're likable, trustworthy, stable, flexible, team-oriented, or a potential red flag.**

send in a message is a data point used by AI to decide whether you're likable, trustworthy, stable, flexible, team-oriented, or a potential red flag.

CREATE A CONSISTENT PERSONALITY PROFILE

To avoid being misread, you must take control of your digital narrative. You must learn to signal the right traits not just in your headline or experience section, but across your whole online presence. This means strategically incorporating elements that signal warmth, openness, humility, and cooperation. It means writing in a tone that sounds like a person, not a robot. It means showing evidence of community involvement, shared values, and team wins. It means remembering that in today's hiring landscape, *perception is prediction*.

In the next chapters, we'll explore exactly how to reshape your LinkedIn presence to match what modern employers, and their machines, are really looking for.

But for now, remember this: you are being profiled. And it's not personal. It's automated.

So, make sure the story it tells is the one you want employers to see.

CHAPTER 22

THE DIGITAL INQUISITION

"You have a reputation score right now. It's already been calculated. You didn't opt in, you can't opt out, and you don't get to see it," I told Daniel and Elaine.

Elaine looked confused. "You mean like a credit score?"

"Exactly," I said. "Except this one measures your professional credibility, influence, and risk profile. And companies can see your score before they ever talk to you."

I explained that every public action — your LinkedIn posts, the groups you join, the endorsements you get, even the consistency between your resume and online profile — feeds into the algorithms that assign you a professional trust score. Recruiters use this score to decide whether you're worth their time. If your score is low, you don't just get fewer interviews, you get fewer callbacks, fewer referrals, and fewer chances, period.

"I never post anything on LinkedIn," Daniel said. "I honestly didn't think that kind of stuff mattered."

"I sometimes comment on posts about controversial news. I assumed that sort of thing would have no impact on my job search," Elaine added.

"It all matters," I told them. "Every click is data."

Daniel, Elaine, and I created a plan for that week to help them rebuild their online profiles: publish two short, relevant posts, post a steady cadence of constructive comments on other people's content, and create alignment between their online profiles and the language of the jobs they wanted.

"You can't see most of these reputation scores or scoring algorithms," I said, "but you can flood the system with the kind of signals that push your scores up."

YOUR SOCIAL MEDIA IS BEING USED TO PREDICT YOUR CANDIDACY

Employers are watching you not just on LinkedIn, but across every digital alleyway you've ever wandered down. Not only are your public social media posts scanned, but so are your old Yelp reviews, anonymous Reddit rants, private Facebook group replies, and even Quora answers from a decade ago.

What does that mean for you as a job seeker, especially an overqualified one who's being scrutinized more than others? It means you must audit your online presence with the same rigor you apply to your resume.

That slightly aggressive product review? It might flag you as disagreeable. The sarcastic tweet? Low Conscientiousness. The ghost town of a LinkedIn profile? Low Extraversion.

According to a Fast Company report, more than 90% of employers now review digital footprints during the hiring process and the absence of a LinkedIn profile alone, or a bare bones LinkedIn profile, can cut your chances of getting an interview in half.[19]

SCRUB BAD POSTS FROM YOUR DIGITAL PRESENCE

AI doesn't need your name to find you anymore. It just needs your words. With linguistic fingerprinting — an advanced forensic technique that analyzes syntax, word choice, and grammatical patterns to trace authorship — AI tools can find you even if you remove your name from your profile. It's the same technique that helped identify the Unabomber.

Today, this technology is being used in education to detect plagiarism and in hiring to identify your anonymous posts. Tools like FLINT Systems and others apply this technology with over 80% accuracy.[20]

The implications are chilling. A candidate rejected after 22 promising interviews finally discovered that a harsh Yelp review from three years earlier that was buried in a dark corner of the internet had been surfaced by AI. Apparently, employers cared about what he'd said in the review. Why? Because companies today are terrified of bad culture fits, and online trolls, even if they're brilliant, pose a retention and PR threat. And when trust is a key currency in any company, one bad apple can cost millions. So, yes, your anonymous negativity might feel like your right, but companies also have the right not to hire you. Courts have repeatedly upheld that freedom of speech does not guarantee employment, especially when that speech reflects poorly on the employer.

> Online trolls, even if they're brilliant, pose a retention and PR threat. And when trust is a key currency in any company, one bad apple can cost millions. So, yes, your anonymous negativity might feel like your right, but companies also have the right not to hire you.

What's the solution? Not to disappear from the internet, that's for sure. Deleting everything, including your LinkedIn, raises its own red flags. Employers are more suspicious of a digital ghost than a digital loudmouth. Instead, take control of your online narrative.

Start by Googling yourself using an incognito browser. Explore the second, third, and fourth pages of results. Search your usernames. See what posts, comments, and profiles show up in the results. Then, clean house.

Delete negative posts. Leave groups that reflect poorly on your professionalism. Replace passive online silence with purposeful branding. Post on LinkedIn. Comment intelligently. Show up like the kind of team member that employers want to bring around the proverbial water cooler.

Your digital fingerprint is part of your application now. And if you're not actively shaping it, someone else's algorithm is doing it for you.

CHAPTER 23

HOW TO FIND AND UNDERSTAND YOUR REPUTATION SCORE

Once Daniel and Elaine grasped the reality of reputation scores, I pulled up LinkedIn's Social Selling Index (SSI). "This is one of the few metrics you can actually see," I told them. "And it's a great indicator of your online reputation. Before we end our meeting today, I want us to look at each of your scores."

Daniel's SSI score was in the low 50s. Elaine's was even lower. "The SSI measures many things. As a user who is not paying for enterprise tools like LinkedIn Recruiter or LinkedIn Talent Solutions, you'll be able to see the basics, namely these four things: how well you established your professional brand, whether or not you are connected to enough of the right people, how much you are engaging appropriately with insights, and how many conversations you're having that build relationships. These are good places to start."

I explained that while SSI was originally designed for companies and salespeople, LinkedIn uses it for all user accounts. "If your SSI is low, it signals that you're disconnected, disengaged, or irrelevant in your space. That's a branding problem," I said.

That afternoon, we spent time tightening their headlines, rewriting their About sections to show potential instead of just past accomplishments, and making sure their skills matched target job descriptions exactly. Then, I had them set a reminder in their calendars to engage with at least one relevant post a day by liking, commenting, or sharing.

Within two weeks, their scores had jumped. A month later, Daniel's score was above 70, and Elaine was close behind.

"Your SSI score is more than a vanity metric," I told them. "It's a proxy for influence and visibility, which get you noticed before you ever apply."

How to See Your Own SSI Score and Start to Influence It

As discussed in the previous chapter, recruiters are using predictive personality modeling and tools like LinkedIn's SSI score to assess your Big Five personality traits and make decisions about your employability before ever speaking to you face-to-face.

To view your own score, start by visiting your Social Selling Index dashboard at https://www.linkedin.com/sales/ssi.

Once on the dashboard, review your score for all four SSI categories:

1. Establish Your Professional Brand
2. Finding the Right People
3. Engage With Insights
4. Build Relationships

From here, you can focus your attention on areas that need improvement. Complete your profile, refine your headline and summary, and start posting thoughtful content once or twice a week. Comment on industry updates and connect with people who reflect your goals. The goal is to build intentional relationships and post with a purpose.

Here are detailed actions you can take to increase your scores in each category:

Establish Your Professional Brand looks at how complete, compelling, and keyword-optimized your profile is. A vague headline like "Experienced Professional" won't help you here. Instead, your headline should answer four key questions: Who are you professionally? Who are you personally? What do you want to do? Where do you want to do it? LinkedIn's algorithm rewards specificity and clarity, so publishing content — whether original posts or shared articles — also helps, particularly when it aligns with the field or roles you're targeting.

Finding the Right People measures how strategic your network is. Having too few connections can make you look isolated. But having too many random connections can dilute your professional identity. LinkedIn rewards meaningful engagement within your desired sector, connecting with people who have the job titles you want, work at the companies you're targeting, or are embedded in your next career move.

The **Engage With Insights** metric evaluates how actively you participate in the professional dialogue happening on LinkedIn. It's not enough to be present, you must be visible. That means reacting to others' posts, commenting thoughtfully, and contributing value. The more you engage with industry-relevant content, the more the algorithm recognizes you as current and credible.

Finally, **Build Relationships** is about depth, not just breadth. The goal is to create a web of authentic, ongoing engagement, not a surface-level collection of connections. Personalized messages, strategic follow-ups, and genuine conversations matter. LinkedIn's system can detect relationship-building behaviors and ranks profiles accordingly.

24-STEP LINKEDIN OPTIMIZATION CHECKLIST FOR OVERQUALIFIED JOB CANDIDATES

For overqualified job seekers, this shift toward the use of digital profiles and algorithm-based personality scores is doubly dangerous. Why? Because traditional cues of experience like long lists of accomplishments, decades-old job titles, or dense resumes, often signal the *wrong* traits — rigidity, overconfidence, or even neuroticism — unless you've taken deliberate steps to humanize and balance your profile.

And this is exactly why LinkedIn now matters more than ever. Not just as your digital resume, but as your psychometric profile.

Fortunately, you *can* influence your reputation score.

To upgrade your LinkedIn profile in a way that positively impacts your reputation score, use this research-backed checklist, adapted from the *Using Available Signals on LinkedIn* study and its accompanying guide, that outlines practical steps to align your digital presence with the traits employers value most.

1. Complete Your Profile

- **Action:** Ensure your LinkedIn profile is complete, including all sections like your headline, summary, experience, education, skills, and photo.
- **Traits Signaled:** Conscientiousness and Extraversion.
- **Notes:** Conscientiousness is one of the best-signaled traits on LinkedIn. A complete profile is a strong indicator of effort and organization, qualities employers value.

2. Write a Long About Section

- **Action:** Craft a LinkedIn Summary that is detailed, professional, summarizing your career goals and achievements.
- **Traits Signaled:** Conscientiousness and Openness.
- **Notes:** Summaries provide a narrative of professional identity, and longer summaries are associated with Conscientiousness, a trait highly desirable in most job roles.

3. Include a Professional Profile Photo

- **Action:** Upload a high-quality, professional headshot as your profile photo.
- **Traits Signaled:** Conscientiousness and Extraversion.
- **Notes:** A photo is a basic expectation on LinkedIn, and its presence aligns with Conscientiousness, which employers prioritize.

4. List More Than Five Skills

- **Action:** Add at least six specific skills to your profile's Skills section that are relevant to your industry or role. Ideally, you should include the maximum number of relevant skills you're allowed to add to the section.
- **Traits Signaled:** Conscientiousness and Extraversion.
- **Notes:** Skills are a key indicator of Conscientiousness, as they require effort to curate and maintain.

5. Obtain at Least Five Endorsements per Skill

- **Action:** Actively seek endorsements from colleagues or connections for your listed skills, aiming for more than five per skill.
- **Traits Signaled:** Extraversion and Conscientiousness.
- **Notes:** Endorsements are stronger signals for Extraversion, as they depend on social connections. This task is especially valuable if you're trying to get a role requiring interpersonal skills.

6. Follow at Least 20 Companies, Groups, and Top Voices

- **Action:** Follow at least 20 companies, industry groups, or professional organizations on LinkedIn.
- **Traits Signaled:** Openness and Extraversion.
- **Notes:** Following companies or groups reflects intellectual curiosity, a hallmark of Openness, which is desirable in creative or innovative roles.

7. List More Than Two Volunteer Experiences

- **Action:** Include at least three volunteer experiences or causes in the Volunteering section of your profile.
- **Traits Signaled:** Agreeableness and Conscientiousness.
- **Notes:** Agreeableness is signaled through prosocial behaviors like volunteering, which employers may value in team-oriented roles.

8. List More Than Two Projects

- **Action:** Add at least three professional or academic projects, with brief descriptions, to the Projects section of your profile.
- **Traits Signaled:** Conscientiousness and Openness.
- **Notes:** Projects signal effort and achievement, which are strongly tied to Conscientiousness, a trait employers universally seek.

9. Include More Than Two Certifications

- **Action:** List at least three professional certifications or courses in the Licenses & Certifications section.
- **Traits Signaled:** Conscientiousness and Openness.
- **Notes:** Certifications are a strong signal of Conscientiousness and a willingness to learn and are particularly relevant for roles requiring specific expertise.

10. Use Positive Emotional Words in Descriptions

- **Action:** Incorporate positive emotional words like *excited*, *passionate*, or *thrilled* in your summary and experience descriptions.
- **Traits Signaled:** Extraversion and Agreeableness.
- **Notes:** Linguistic cues like positive emotional words align with Extraversion and help counter signals of Neuroticism, which employers typically view negatively.

11. Avoid Negative Emotional Words

- **Action:** Refrain from using negative emotional words like *stressed*, *frustrated*, or *disappointed* in any profile section.
- **Traits Signaled:** Neuroticism.
- **Notes:** Negative words increase signals of emotional instability. Instead, use positive emotional words to present a stable, professional image and suggest cooperation.

12. Use Achievement-Oriented Language

- **Action:** Describe experiences using action verbs and achievement-oriented terms like *led*, *achieved*, or *delivered* in job descriptions.
- **Traits Signaled:** Conscientiousness and Extraversion.
- **Notes:** Language that highlights accomplishments is a key trait signaling employability.

13. Have More Than 500 Connections

- **Action:** Build your network to exceed 500 LinkedIn connections. Your goal should be to reach at least 2,000 connections with relevant professionals.
- **Traits Signaled:** Extraversion and Conscientiousness.
- **Notes:** A large network size suggests Extraversion, which is critical for roles involving collaboration or client interaction because it signals sociability and networking skills.

14. Include Education Details

- **Action:** Fully complete your Education section with degrees, institutions, and relevant coursework or honors.
- **Traits Signaled:** Conscientiousness and Openness.
- **Notes:** Not only do these elements expand your network and therefore imply Extraversion, but the institutions you list will automatically connect you with other alumni.

15. List More Than Two Publications

- **Action:** Add at least three publications (e.g., articles, reports, or papers) to the Publications section, if applicable.
- **Traits Signaled:** Openness and Conscientiousness.
- **Notes:** Sharing the publications you're interested in shows you're keeping tabs on the industry and is another opportunity to highlight topics you're interested in outside of work.

16. Include "Curiosity" as One of Your Skills

- **Action:** Specifically list *curiosity* or a related term, like *inquisitiveness*, in your Skills section.
- **Traits Signaled:** Openness.
- **Notes:** Curiosity implies Openness and reinforces intellectual engagement.

17. Share Professional Posts or Articles

- **Action:** Regularly post or share content about industry insights, achievements, or professional topics.
- **Traits Signaled:** Extraversion and Openness.
- **Notes:** Active engagement signals Extraversion and sharing content reflects intellectual curiosity.

18. Describe Your Achievements in Your Work Experience

- **Action:** Add specific achievements like "Increased sales by 20%" to each job you have listed in the Experiences section.
- **Traits Signaled:** Conscientiousness and Extraversion.
- **Notes:** Highlighting results shows diligence and confidence.

19. Use First-Person Pronouns

- **Action:** Write your summary and descriptions using "I statements" like "I led a team," where appropriate.

- **Traits Signaled:** Extraversion and Openness.
- **Notes:** First-person pronouns reflect self-confidence and personal engagement, aligning with Extraversion.

20. Add Honors and Awards

- **Action:** List any professional or academic awards in the Honors and Awards section.
- **Traits Signaled:** Conscientiousness and Openness.
- **Notes:** Similar to projects or certifications, awards reflect effort and recognition.

21. Include Recommendations

- **Action:** Request at least one written recommendation from a colleague or supervisor.
- **Traits Signaled:** Extraversion and Agreeableness.
- **Notes:** Recommendations, like endorsements, depend on social relationships, signaling sociability and likability.

22. Customize Your LinkedIn URL

- **Action:** Change your LinkedIn URL to a clean, professional format like linkedin.com/in/yourname.
- **Traits Signaled:** Conscientiousness.
- **Notes:** Having a complete profile is critical, and a customized URL shows attention to detail.

23. Update Your Profile Regularly

- **Action:** Periodically add new skills, experiences, or certifications to keep your profile current.
- **Traits Signaled:** Conscientiousness and Openness.
- **Notes:** Regular updates signal ongoing effort and adaptability.

24. Engage with Others' Content

- **Action:** Like, comment, or share posts from your network or industry leaders.
- **Traits Signaled:** Extraversion and Openness.
- **Notes:** Active networking and connections signal Extraversion, and engagement shows interest in others' ideas.

BECOME THE BEST-FIT CANDIDATE

Your SSI score is just the beginning of the data available about who you are online. Behind the curtain, employer platforms like LinkedIn Recruiter and LinkedIn Talent Solutions leverage hundreds of additional data points to score you even further.

The end game of all this profiling isn't sinister; it's *efficiency*. Employers are flooded with applications. They're using every tool available to reduce candidates to numbers. Whether they admit it or not, the question they're asking isn't "Can you do the job?" It's "What does your data say about who you are?"

And unless you take control of your data, the number they assign you may not reflect your potential; it may simply reflect your past. Or worse, your silence.

So, as we move into the next chapters, remember that employers aren't just reviewing your resume. They're profiling your personality. And unless you deliberately craft your digital footprint to align with what employers seek — traits like Conscientiousness, Agreeableness, and Extraversion — you risk being filtered out because you failed to manage the signals that inform your reputation score.

CHAPTER 24

COMMENTS ARE THE NEW COVER LETTER

Elaine gave me a skeptical look and said, "You mean just typing a comment under someone's post is as important as a cover letter?"

"In many cases, more important," I said. "Your comments are public. They live on that post and are visible to the poster's entire network, including recruiters and decision-makers."

"I still don't understand how that works," Elaine said.

"A thoughtful comment on the right post can work like a warm introduction," I said. "It shows your voice, your thinking, and your ability to add value to a conversation. And unlike a cover letter, it doesn't get buried in an Applicant Tracking System."

As part of Elaine and Daniel's roadmap for rehabilitating their online profiles, they committed to finding three posts from leaders, hiring managers, or influential employees at their target companies and commenting one or two sentences that connected the post to their own expertise or asked a thoughtful question.

Daniel commented on a VP's post about emerging industry trends, adding a short case study from his experience. Elaine congratulated a target company on a successful product launch and asked about lessons learned during development.

Both received direct replies. "See?" I said. "You're no longer a stranger on the internet. You're a voice they recognize. You can also now name-drop these contacts in future cover letters, as we've discussed."

By now, you understand that employers aren't just reading your resume, they're profiling *you*. Not the you on paper, but the you in motion: your clicks, your searches, your likes, your silence. If you think you're applying to jobs behind a curtain, think again. Employers today are watching everything, especially on LinkedIn.

That's why the most overlooked, underutilized, and wildly powerful way to break into the job market today isn't submitting another application. It's *commenting*. Thoughtful, targeted commenting on the content published by companies you want to work for is no longer optional. It's a strategic move to build connection and increase visibility.

I'M DYING TO WORK FOR YOU, BUT I IGNORE YOUR COMPANY PAGE COMPLETELY

LinkedIn Recruiter, the tool used by nearly every medium-to-large company to find candidates, reveals far more than you think. Employers can see if you've followed their company, liked or shared their posts, commented on anything they've published, and even whether you've engaged with any of their employees. That gushing message you sent to the recruiter about how much you admire the company's work rings hollow if you haven't even scrolled their feed.

They know you haven't. And they're not impressed.

For overqualified job seekers, engaging with a company's LinkedIn content is even more important. Why? Because, as we talked about in previous chapters, you already carry a risk profile in the eyes of many employers. Your digital behavior can either confirm those fears or extinguish them.

Engagement, especially in the form of comments, is your way to show employers that you're not applying randomly. It's proof you're paying attention. And companies are begging for that kind of signal. When a company posts about a new initiative, service, or internal culture update, they're looking for feedback. These are posts that are often curated by communications teams and monitored by recruiters, marketing leads, and HR stakeholders. These are the people who decide who gets interviewed. They notice who engages. They know who's lurking, who's passive, and who's tuned in.

Even more specifically, internal recruiters (yes, the very people who may be reviewing your resume resume) are often required to post about open roles and company culture from their personal LinkedIn profiles. That means they're not just on LinkedIn scrolling; they're *tracking*. They're held accountable to engagement metrics. And when you interact with their posts, you become someone with initiative and name recognition.

HOW TO GET STARTED COMMENTING AND SHOWING ENGAGEMENT

If you haven't already completed the LinkedIn Optimization Checklist in Chapter 23, go back and do that first. Then, once on LinkedIn, follow every company you've applied to, are planning to apply to, or even just admire. Look at their last month of posts. Click "like" on a few that resonate. Then take the next step and leave a short, intelligent comment. You don't need to write a novel. A single sentence is enough if it shows you understand what the company is doing and why it matters.

For example:

- "Love how you're addressing [industry trend]. It's clear your team is staying ahead of the curve."
- "Excited to see this kind of innovation coming out of [company name], really aligns with what I value in an organization."
- "Great post. As someone focused on [area of expertise], it's inspiring to see your team prioritize this work."

And don't stop at the company page. Seek out hiring managers, department leads, and relevant employees, especially those who work in the department you're targeting. Connect with them (with a short note) and engage with their content too. The more you show up on their radar in small, value-driven ways, the more they'll notice when your resume hits their desk.

This strategy works for anyone, but it's *crucial* for the overqualified. You need to counter the narrative that you're disinterested, outdated, or opportunistic. And commenting is how you demonstrate you're *present*, curious, aligned, and ready to contribute, not just capable, but *invested*.

CHAPTER 25

THE HIDDEN POWER OF WEAK TIES AND WORKPLACE ALUMNI

When I told Daniel that his next opportunity was more likely to come from someone he barely knew than from a close friend, he laughed. "That makes no sense," he said.

"It makes perfect sense," I said. "Your close network knows all the same people and opportunities you do. Weak ties open new circles."

"Are you sure?" Elaine asked. "I haven't reached out to anyone from my last three jobs. Maybe I could send some of them a message to let them know I'm looking for a new position."

"I don't want to bother people I haven't spoken to in years," Daniel said.

"People generally like to help — especially if you shared a workplace, a project, or even just an industry connection," I said. "Let's start by building a list of former colleagues, past vendors, and old managers. Then we'll craft short, friendly messages that reference your shared experience and ask how they've been. At this point, you're not asking for a job, you're just rekindling the connection."

A week later, Elaine got coffee with a former coworker who introduced her to a department head at a target company. Daniel reconnected with a supplier contact who offered to pass along his resume internally.

"These aren't favors," I told them. "They're the natural result of keeping weak ties alive. Every touchpoint is a door you might walk through later."

WHY FORMER WORK COLLEAGUES GIVE THE BEST REFERRALS

Your inner circle is rarely the group of people that helps you get hired. Yes, they want you to land another role, but it's usually the folks on the edges of your network — the people you *used to* work with or went to school with but haven't spoken to in years — who hold the keys to your next career move.

A massive, five-year experiment conducted by MIT and LinkedIn involving 20 million users, more than 70 million job applications, and more than 600,000 accepted positions revealed that the weaker the connection between users, the more likely it led to a new job.[21] As the study's authors put it, "the stronger the newly added ties were, the less likely they were to lead to a job transmission."

In fact, it was the "moderately weak ties" — people with whom you share about 10 mutual connections on LinkedIn — that created the highest probability of landing a job. Not your best friends. Not your former boss. Not your sibling's colleague. It was the second- or third-degree contact you haven't spoken to for three years who ended up being the magic bridge.

The MIT and LinkedIn researchers broke "tie strength" down in two ways: structural and interactive. Structurally, weak ties are people with whom you share few mutual connections. Interactively, they're the ones you rarely message or engage with. And yet, these less familiar contacts were the most effective at getting people hired. Why? Because they expose you to new information, new opportunities, and new introductions your close contacts simply don't have access to.

In a separate study that examined more than 380 job success stories, researchers found that former workplace contacts, especially former colleagues, bosses, and even clients, accounted for over 60% of all successful referrals. Compare that to just 17% who landed jobs through other weak ties.[22]

What these former coworkers offer isn't just a foot in the door, but something rarer: *proof.* Proof that you're competent. Proof that you're collaborative. Proof that you're not too senior, too rusty, or too expensive.

TAP INTO LINKEDIN'S DIGITAL GOLDMINE

Now here's where things get really interesting. LinkedIn was built for this exact kind of triangulation, and yet, most job seekers aren't using it strategically. They're chasing the people they know best, instead of the alumni and ex-coworkers they haven't connected with in years.

This is your wake-up call. You don't need to wait for a friend to refer you. You need to tap into the digital goldmine already under your feet: the LinkedIn Alumni Tool.

Every university you've attended (and as an overqualified professional, you've likely attended two or more) has a searchable, filterable list of graduates across industries, companies, job titles, and locations. These aren't just people with something in common; they're people who are preconditioned to want to help you.

Schools have spent millions reinforcing the power of the alumni network. These connections don't require a shared major, graduation year, or mutual friend. A shared school name is enough to open a conversation, spark a referral, or build a bridge to someone who can walk your resume into the hiring manager's office.

To get started, click on the "Alumni" tab on your university's LinkedIn page. Filter users by location, industry, and company. See who's working at the organizations you're targeting. Then send a brief, direct message. Keep it short and be human. Say something like, "Hi [Name], I saw your recent post on LinkedIn about [topic] and noticed we're both alumni of [University]. I also saw you're working at [Company] in [job title] role. Congratulations on your success. If you're open to connecting, I'd love to stay in touch."

That's it. You don't need to ask for a referral on the first message. You just need to start the conversation. That's how modern job seeking works. You're not begging strangers for jobs or spamming resumes into black boxes. You're engaging the people who are close enough to care and far enough to help.

This strategy works even better when it overlaps with the digital reputation and engagement techniques you've already read about in previous chapters. When you comment on someone's post before you message them or follow the company page before you request an intro, it creates a halo effect that makes you appear visible, familiar, and engaged. By the time you show up in their inbox, you're not a stranger, you're someone they've seen, like, and maybe even respect.

> **When you comment on someone's post before you message them or follow the company page before you request an intro, it creates a halo effect that makes you appear visible, familiar, and engaged.**

In the next chapter, we'll take this a step further and break down exactly how to craft these outreach messages, what *not* to say, and how to stack your weak ties and alumni connections into a referral pipeline that quietly does the heavy lifting for you.

But for now, remember this: the people who are most likely to help you get hired aren't your best friends or your current coworkers. They're the ones you used to know. And it's time to reintroduce yourself.

CHAPTER 26

SAY SOMETHING ABOUT *THEM* FIRST

Elaine and Daniel's applications started gaining traction. They had interviews lined up and more positions they wanted to apply for. But they hadn't been networking nearly enough. So, we met to discuss how to initiate some conversations and how to create some weak, but not too weak, connections.

Most outreach messages fail because they start with "I" or "me," so when Daniel drafted a note that began, "I'm looking for my next role" I stopped him.

"Flip it," I said. "Start by focusing on *them*. You have to make your comments specific, genuine, and relevant."

Elaine's first message was to a hiring manager at a company she admired. She opened with, "I saw your team recently launched the GreenTech initiative — congratulations. That's a major step toward sustainable operations." Only then did she briefly introduce herself and ask about the project.

Daniel messaged a former industry peer and said, "I just read your article on supply chain resilience — insightful work, especially your point about nearshoring." His message turned into a 20-minute call that ended with an offer to forward his resume internally.

"When you start with them," I told them, "you lower defenses and increase engagement. People remember those who notice their work."

A CONNECTION REQUEST IS LAZY IF IT DOESN'T COME WITH THE RIGHT MESSAGE

Most people on LinkedIn don't know how to send a cold outreach message. They copy and paste the same bland message to everyone, and they lead with their resume, their story, their struggles. They open cold connections with essays about their background, or worse, send no message at all. And then they sit back and wonder why no one replies.

But the real reason you're being ignored has nothing to do with your qualifications. It's because you've asked someone to give you something, time, attention, advice, a referral, without giving them anything first.

Today's job market is flooded with automated outreach, scams, and bots. No one has time to wade through generic requests. That means if you want to stand out, your first message has to cut through the noise. And that starts with a sentence about *them*.

The moment someone posts something publicly on LinkedIn, whether it's a short update, a shared article, or a celebration of their team, they're sending a subtle but powerful signal that says, "I want to be seen." That post exists because they want engagement. And when you acknowledge it with sincerity, when you quote it, comment on it, or explain why it stood out to you, you tap into the powerful psychological force of reciprocity.

Reciprocity is one of the oldest principles in human persuasion. People are hardwired to respond positively to kindness, especially when it feels unexpected. When someone feels seen, they're more likely to see you in return. When someone feels heard, they're more likely to listen. That's why the first line of any cold outreach message should sound like this:

"Hey [Name], I just read your post about [topic], and I really appreciated what you said about [specific detail]."

That's it. You're not asking for a job. You're not dumping your entire work history on them. You're simply being human. And in doing so, you earn a moment of trust — the most valuable currency in a job search.

> Reciprocity is one of the oldest principles in human persuasion. People are hardwired to respond positively to kindness, especially when it feels unexpected. When someone feels seen, they're more likely to see you in return.

Every recruiter, hiring manager, and gatekeeper on LinkedIn has been burned by timewasters. They've been pitched by fake profiles, spammed by bots, and ghosted by opportunists. So, when your message hits their inbox, the first thing they think is, *Who is this person? What do they want? Are they going to waste my time? Are they an AI bot?*

YOU'RE NOT AN AI AGENT, SO DON'T ACT LIKE ONE

If you start your message with yourself, your resume, your needs, your ambition, the person you're trying to connect with will shut down. But if your message opens with something that makes *them* feel acknowledged and appreciated, their brain does something different. It doesn't brace for a pitch. It leans in. It opens the door.

That's all you need: a door slightly ajar. Because once they respond, once they know you're a real, thoughtful, professional human being, the next steps become much easier. That response can lead to a conversation. That conversation can lead to a referral. And a referral can lead to a job offer — sometimes one that never even got posted. But none of that happens if you don't master the art of crafting a first sentence about *them*.

FIND THEIR EMAIL ADDRESS AND REACH OUT ON TWO FRONTS

You should be using LinkedIn Messenger to send these kinds of messages, especially after commenting on someone's post. But you shouldn't stop there. Messages sent via email still have a far higher read and response rate than LinkedIn InMails or connection requests. And most of the time, getting someone's email address is surprisingly easy.

Start with tools like Hunter.io, which lets you search by domain name (like @company.com) and provides verified email formats. Another great option is RocketReach, which offers both emails and social handles with confidence scores. You can also try ContactOut, which integrates directly with LinkedIn to help find professional email addresses.

But even without tools, many company email addresses follow predictable formats:

- firstname.lastname@company.com
- firstinitiallastname@company.com
- firstname_lastname@company.com
- firstname@company.com

If you know the name of the person and the domain of their company's email, you're already halfway there. Use LinkedIn to find the right names. Use the company website to find the domain. Then test the most common permutations.

And once you have their email, don't send a wall of text. Use the exact same approach as you would when sending a direct message on LinkedIn: one or two short sentences about them, what you noticed, and why you're reaching out. Then end with an invitation to talk, not a demand.

Remember that your goal in all of this is to feel like a *colleague*, not a *cold caller*. A real person, not a resume. And the easiest, fastest way to build that rapport, whether online or in person, is to notice someone first.

That's how you go from invisible to interesting. That's how you get hired.

CHAPTER 27

FROM STRANGER TO REFERRAL: THE FOUR LEVELS OF PROFESSIONAL INTIMACY

"You can't cold message someone and expect them to put their name on the line for you," I told Daniel and Elaine. "There's a process to building a relationship with someone you've never met before."

I made a list of the four levels of professional relationships on the whiteboard in the corner of my office:

1. Stranger
2. Acquaintance
3. Professional Contact
4. Trusted Advocate

Elaine realized most of her outreach jumped from Level 1 to Level 4 in a single email... and failed. Daniel admitted he'd been doing the same.

Now that they had a better understanding of *why* their current outreach efforts were falling short, we rebuilt their networking approach. The plan was to engage with someone's content first (Level 1 to 2), share value or insights over time (Level 2 to 3), then — when there's rapport — ask for a call or introduction (Level 3 to 4).

This slower, layered approach meant fewer awkward rejections and more genuine yeses.

"By the time you ask for a referral," I told them, "it should feel like the next logical step, not a leap of faith."

REFERRALS AREN'T JUST HELPFUL, THEY'RE TRANSFORMATIVE

A single referral can allow you to skip multiple rounds of a hiring process, reopen a previously rejected application, or even override an internal objection. For overqualified job seekers who are often misunderstood, having someone advocate for you inside a company can be the game-changer you need.

But how do you actually get someone to refer you? Not with a cold message, not with a PDF resume, and not by dropping the words "I'm job searching" into a stranger's DMs. You get a referral by building trust, and that means building what's called *professional intimacy*.

In fact, there's a specific, research-backed path for deepening rapport and transforming new or distant LinkedIn contacts into advocates. This path consists of four levels of growing professional connection. Done right, it mirrors how real-world conversations naturally evolve when trust is built thoughtfully.

Level 1: What Are You Working on That You're Excited About?

The first level of connection is light, friendly, and professional. It's about giving your contact the opportunity to share something positive about themselves, their current role, a recent project, or an aspect of their job that energizes them. The best entry question is simple and effective:

"What are you working on right now that you're excited about?"

This sets a casual tone and allows them to feel seen and appreciated. Don't jump into your own goals or pitch yet. This phase is about *them*, not you. Other effective questions at this level include:

- "What's a typical day like in your role?"
- "What do you enjoy most about what you do?"
- "What surprised you about your role when you started?"

As behavioral science research published in the Harvard Business Review shows asking thoughtful, positive questions not only builds trust but also makes you more likable.[23] In one study conducted by psychologists Arthur Aron and Alison Wood Brooks, participants rated conversation partners who asked more questions — particularly follow-up questions — as significantly more enjoyable to talk to. That means the first step in getting noticed is making the other person feel heard.

Level 2: What Challenges Come with That Work?

Once you've established a little rapport, you can move gently to the second level of intimacy. This step involves asking about the challenges they face, demonstrating empathy and respect for their expertise.

A strong question to transition here is:

"That sounds like a really dynamic project. I imagine it comes with challenges. What are some you're facing right now?"

Now the tone deepens. You're showing that you're not just interested in their wins, but also their grit. You're recognizing them as a problem-solver. Additional follow-up questions include:

- "What kinds of skills do you find yourself relying on most often?
- "How do you approach those challenges?"
- "What do you find most difficult but rewarding?"

This mirrors findings from Aron and Brooks' research on cooperative conversations. By asking meaningful questions and actively listening to answers, participants were more liked, retained more information, and were more likely to be invited to future discussions. Basically, when you show genuine curiosity, not for manipulation, but for understanding, you unlock connection.

Level 3: How Did You Get Hired There?

With credibility and comfort building, you can move into the third level of connection and ask about their personal journey. This is where many professionals easily open up about their own job search because the spotlight stays on them and what they experienced. This also primes them for you to ask about your job search next. A great question to ask in this level is "How did you get hired into your role in the first place?"

Other questions include:

- "What did your hiring process look like?"
- "Was there anything that helped you stand out as a candidate?"
- "How has your career evolved since joining the company?"

These experience-based questions signal that you see them not only as someone doing a great job now, but someone whose story you can learn from. As the studies from Aron and Brooks showed, when conversations start shallow and gradually deepen, like this process does, rapport and trust are built far more quickly. In fact, people who followed this progression in experiments were significantly more likely to want to meet again, even after a single conversation.

Level 4: Are There Any Opportunities in the Pipeline?

Only after you've gone through the first three stages of connection should you pivot toward talking about your own professional goals. And even then, you should do it *gently* by linking it to their story and expertise. For example:

"I had no idea that your interview process involved three video rounds, that's really insightful. I've been looking at roles in companies like yours. Do you know if there are any openings coming up in your department or elsewhere in the company?"

You can also ask:

- "Would you be open to reviewing my resume?"
- "Would you be comfortable passing it along if you think I'm a good fit?"
- "Is there someone else I should talk to who knows more about hiring for [specific department]?"

You're not pushing, you're opening a door that they may want to walk through. If the connection is strong, they'll often offer help without being asked.

CLOSE THE CONVERSATION WITH RECIPROCATION

At this point, you've given them attention, listened deeply, and made them feel valued. And that gives them a reason to return the favor. Behavioral economists have shown that people are more likely to help someone they've bonded with, even in small ways, because it activates a basic reciprocity reflex.[24]

If they can't refer you directly, ask a soft, casual follow-up:

"Would you be open to introducing me to someone else who might have more insight into that area?"

This request is low-pressure, but it creates a powerful network effect. It turns one conversation into two, then three, then five. And this is how most people break into their next role — through someone who knows someone.

Building professional intimacy doesn't mean being manipulative. It means showing up with curiosity, humility, and generosity. Ask more questions. Listen longer. And when you finally do talk about yourself, people will want to hear more.

Referrals don't come from luck; they come from strategy and empathy.

SECTION FOUR

FROM GETTING INTERVIEWS TO PASSING INTERVIEWS

CHAPTER 28

CULTURE FIT IS THE ONLY INTERVIEW ASSESSMENT

By our fourth week together, Daniel and Elaine were ready to start thinking about the interview stage of the hiring process. I started our meeting by reminding them that in today's job market, culture matters more than competence.

Daniel raised an eyebrow. "Surely skills and experience matter more than culture fit. I know we talked about removing the perception of risk by targeting our resumes and cover letters, but we have to think about this in an interview too?"

"Yes, you do," I said. "Culture fit is the number one deciding factor after you've cleared the basic qualifications. If they don't think you'll mesh with their team, you're done."

Elaine admitted she'd spent most interviews trying to prove her expertise. "I thought that was what they wanted."

"It's not enough," I said. "They're asking themselves if they want to work with you every day. They want to know if you'll make their job easier or harder. Just like with your resume and cover letter, your perceived culture fit in an interview often predicts hiring decisions better than experience does."

Then, we worked on subtle cues like mirroring communication styles, using the company's own language, and referencing their values naturally in conversation. Daniel practiced smiling more in mock interviews, and Elaine toned down technical jargon and focused on shared goals.

"Culture fit isn't about being fake," I told them. "It's about showing you can thrive in their environment."

There are only two problems you'll encounter in the job market: either you're not getting enough interviews, or you're not getting job offers after the interviews you do get. Occasionally, both are happening to you.

Everything we've covered up to now has focused on solving the first problem: getting noticed, getting past the filters, and getting in the room. Now, it's time to solve the second one.

SHOW THE HIRING MANAGER THAT YOU'RE THE BEST CULTURE FIT

Unfortunately, most people — whether they're highly qualified or not — think the interview is about them. They assume that if they show their skills, talk about their background, and keep it professional, they'll impress the hiring manager. But the hiring manager doesn't care about your background (if you weren't qualified, you wouldn't have been invited in for an interview). They care about one thing: keeping their job. And their job depends on whether you, the person they hire, will stay for at least two years. That's the metric that matters.

Will I get fired by hiring you? is the question ringing in the hiring manager's ears when you

> Will I get fired by hiring you? is the question ringing in the hiring manager's ears when you walk into the interview room.

CULTURE FIT IS THE ONLY INTERVIEW ASSESSMENT

walk into the interview room. If you think they care about your credentials more than their own survival, you've already lost.

The hiring manager is never going to tell you this. Instead, when they choose someone else for the position, they'll say something generic like, "We went with someone whose experience was a better fit," or, "We chose a candidate with more relevant background."

These sound like good reasons, but they're both a lie. Hiring managers use these platitudes because if they said what they really thought — *We didn't think you'd stick around*, or *You didn't seem like you'd fit in with the team* — they'd risk a lawsuit.

The real assessment that's happening during an interview, is whether you seem like you'll stay. And the only reliable signal of your potential tenure with the company is how well the hiring manager thinks you'll fit in with their existing culture.

Employers won't directly ask, "Do you think you'd be a good cultural fit?" That's too legally risky. Instead, they'll say things like, "What kind of team do you like to work on?" or, "What sort of environment brings out your best?"

Basically, do you seem like someone who belongs here, someone who gets us, someone who will still be here two years from now? If the answer is yes, you have a shot. If the answer is no, you're out, no matter how good your resume is. If you miss these culture-screening questions or if you go off onto some tangent about your project management style or past performance metrics, you're finished.

Fortunately (or unfortunately), you can't fake this with a script. Hiring managers do 10 interviews a day. They've heard every cliché, every line, and every robotic answer. They're walking bullshit detectors. You say, "I see myself here for the next five years," and they nod and smile, then mark you as a no because they've heard it a thousand times. What they're actually listening for is how you talk about teams, how you talk about challenges, how you talk about why you applied. They're reading between the lines.

CULTURE FIT INDICATES RETENTION, AND RETENTION IS GOOD FOR HIRING MANAGERS

Let's put some real numbers on this. According to Deloitte, 88% of job seekers and 94% of business owners believe a healthy workplace culture is vital to success.[25] And companies with strong, aligned cultures experience up to 30% less turnover, according to Glassdoor data.[26]

Conversely, bad hires who don't fit cost companies between 50% and 200% of the employee's annual salary in replacement costs and productivity loss.[27] That's why companies invest millions in "culture fit assessments," pre-employment behavioral evaluations, and even AI personality testing. The hiring process may look like it's about skills, but under the hood, it's all about whether or not you'll stay with the company.

And here's why hiring managers care so much about finding the person who's the right fit: they're being evaluated, sometimes by algorithms, based on the retention rate of the people they bring in.

Every hiring manager is judged on how long the people they hire stay with the company. If you leave before 24 months, they're in trouble. Their boss looks at them like they failed. Their bonus disappears. They may not get promoted. They could lose their job, which means they'll lose their health insurance, and their kids' tuition payments might bounce. If the next person they hire quits within their industry-standard, two-year retention goal, their record is tainted.

So, ask yourself: if your job depended on hiring someone who you knew would stay for two years minimum, what would you care about most? A glowing resume? Fancy credentials? No. You'd care whether this person would actually like the team, vibe with the boss, and show up motivated. You'd care about cultural alignment, because misalignment is a guaranteed exit.

Still skeptical? A Chapman & Co. study shows that interviewers make up their minds about cultural fit within the first three minutes of an interview.[28] Once they decide whether you're going to mesh with the company, they spend the rest of the interview confirming what their gut has already told them. Think about how fragile that is. Now think about how crucial it is to understand what they're really scanning for.

HOW TO STUDY AND MATCH A COMPANY'S CULTURE SO YOU DON'T HAVE TO FAKE IT TO MAKE IT

Most people completely overestimate how well they interview. While you are likely very skilled in your work domain, you are likely *not* skilled in the domain of interviewing. Yet, the majority of job candidates I have worked with strongly believe they are superior interviewees. This overestimation effect is called the Dunning-Kruger effect, and it is very dangerous for your job search.[29]

Why does this effect happen? Because job seekers are focused on themselves. They're nervous, they're stressed, and they're obsessed with proving they're good enough. But the interview isn't about proving anything. It's about aligning. It's about making the hiring manager feel like choosing you is the safest, smartest thing they can do for their career.

In particular, trying to "play it cool" doesn't work. Acting aloof, pretending you don't need the job, or giving off that detached, too-calm energy, kills your candidacy. The hiring manager wants to see your hunger, humility, and a willingness to do what it takes to commit and contribute.

You need to show that you want this job more than anything, that you respect what the company is doing, and that you see this as a privilege, not a steppingstone. It's better to be so hungry for the job that you feel desperate and get hired because of that than to play it cool and stay unemployed.

> Acting aloof, pretending you don't need the job, or giving off that detached, too-calm energy, kills your candidacy. The hiring manager wants to see your hunger, humility, and a willingness to do what it takes to commit and contribute.

So, how do you show the interviewer that you're a good culture fit?

First, stop thinking your skills and experience will save you. They won't. Not on their own.

Second, study the company's values. Not the ones on the career page, the ones in their employee reviews, social media posts, LinkedIn profiles, and team bios. Mirror that language in your answers. If the company cares about humility, don't brag. If they prize collaboration, talk about how you work cross-functionally. And don't just say "I'm passionate about this company," show it by engaging with their content, learning their language, and mentioning specific things you admire.

Third, and most importantly, be real. The same Chapman & Co. study found that some candidates who *aren't* a good fit can keep up a facade for three to six months before their true style shows, and a bad culture fit wrecks teams. Employers know this, and it's why they'd rather take someone with slightly less technical ability and the right mindset than someone with a perfect resume who's secretly a misfit.

This matters for you, too, because if you fake a culture fit just to get the job, you'll end up miserable again. You'll dread Mondays. You'll fight subtle friction all day. And you'll leave and have to start all over again. So be honest. But also, be intentional. Learn the culture. Speak to it. Sell your alignment as hard as you sell your skills.

In the next two chapters, I'll introduce you to cross-generational and cross-educational relatability and the two questions that employers ask during every interview to determine cultural fit. After reading them, you will be prepared to prove why you're the best person for the job.

CHAPTER 29

CAN YOU SIT AT EVERY TABLE?

Elaine admitted she'd been feeling out of place in interviews with younger hiring managers. "They probably see me as old-fashioned," she said.

Daniel had the opposite issue. He felt over-educated compared to peers without degrees.

This generational and experiential gap is something many of my clients' experience. Fortunately, much of the work Daniel and Elaine had done to increase their levels of agreeableness and likability in their resumes and cover letters could be carried over to the interview experience.

"As a highly qualified candidate who's already had a long and successful career, sitting at an interview table with people who are younger and less experienced than you are unavoidable. But adaptability across generations and education levels is a huge advantage if you demonstrate it," I said.

As usual, Elaine looked relieved, and Daniel still seemed skeptical.

"If you come across as dismissive of other backgrounds, even unintentionally," I said, "you'll be ruled out."

To make sure Elaine and Daniel would be prepared to engage with interviewers, no matter their age, we practiced conversational bridges — how to reference experience without making it sound like a lecture and how to ask questions that showed genuine curiosity about different perspectives.

Watching my parents struggle had made me hyper-aware of how small social cues could close doors. My dad once said, "Back in my day...," in an interview, and he came home and told my mom that the atmosphere in the room instantly cooled — a story I'd heard many of my career coaching clients repeat.

"Making cross-generational connections isn't about hiding your background; it's about showing you can work alongside anyone, regardless of age or education," I told them.

By our next mock interview, Daniel was relating his Six Sigma expertise to the fresh problem-solving approaches of Gen Z hires, and Elaine was connecting her leadership style to managers who had never worked outside tech. Both were learning to sit at every table.

ARE YOU FAILING THE WATER COOLER TEST?

One of the reasons most overqualified job candidates don't get hired today is because of how their credentials make hiring managers feel. If you have a master's degree or multiple master's degrees, if you're over 40, especially if you're over 50 or 60, and if you have more than 20 years of experience with previous titles like Senior Vice President or Director, most employers don't think, *Wow, what a capable candidate*, they think, *This person probably can't relate to the rest of my team.*

They're not wondering if you can lead cross-functionally (they already assume you can), but they *do* want to know you can work cross-generationally and cross-educationally.

You're focused on proving you're good enough for the job, but the hiring manager is wondering if you'll make their team uncomfortable. They're wondering if the 21-year-old working the help desk is going to roll their eyes when you start a sentence with, "Back when I was at [insert previous company]." They're wondering if their 28-year-old rising star in sales is going to feel like they suddenly have a helicopter parent hovering nearby. Or if their team with mostly bachelor's degrees is going to feel like you look down on them when you leverage your big vocabulary with "executive presence."

The real litmus test for determining whether you can sit at every table is the water cooler test.

Basically, does the hiring manager think you'd be able to hold a five-minute conversation by the break room coffee pot or water cooler with someone decades younger or who didn't go to college and still make that person feel seen, respected, and equal?

Unfortunately, most candidates who've spent years in leadership or high-responsibility roles have no idea how to pass the water cooler test.

Most hiring managers have already witnessed what happens when an impressive hire comes in and immediately creates a status gap inside the team. Suddenly, entry-level employees stop speaking up, the informal culture dies, collaboration breaks down, the team starts holding back in meetings, and the work gets worse, not better.

In this job market, where every team is stretched and burnout is high, emotional safety matters more than credentials. As a result, your ability to connect across generational and educational divides is not a nice-to-have, it's the number one concern a hiring manager has when reviewing your background if you're overqualified. Showing you're capable of meeting your potential future peers (and the hiring manager) at their level is therefore a top priority during an interview.

REPLACE TEACHING AND COACHING WITH COLLABORATION AND CONNECTION

In today's workforce, it's not uncommon for executives to report to people ten or twenty years younger than them. If you're a candidate in your 50s, you may be interviewing with someone who was in high school when you were managing a multimillion-dollar budget. If you don't go out of your way to neutralize the power imbalance your resume creates, it will likely cost you the job offer.

Talking too much about your history, titles, past impact, and degrees and not enough about how you think you'll fit into your new team is where most experienced and educated job candidates sabotage themselves without realizing it. If you speak in structured, formal way that sounds great in a board meeting but lands awkwardly in a casual team setting or if you default to teaching rather than collaborating, you're posturing instead of connecting.

And while hiring managers will smile and nod, maybe even say, "we'll be in touch," they can immediately feel the disconnect and the decision has already been made. You won't be invited back. Not because you weren't smart enough. But because you didn't make them feel like you belonged with the people already on their team.

So, what can you do?

If you've worked with someone in their 20s who taught you about a new app or sales tactic, bring that up. If you've been part of a team where everyone had different levels of education, talk about how you adapted your communication style to make sure everyone understood and contributed equally. If you've reported to someone younger or worked under a new system that clashed with your instincts, but you still made it work, share that story. You must make it unmistakably clear that you are coachable, collaborative, and culturally fluid.

CHAPTER 30

WHY YOU? WHY US? THE TWO QUESTIONS THAT DECIDE EVERYTHING

Just like the work you did to target your cover letter to appeal to a specific company, all interviews boil down to how well you can answer these two questions:

1. Why you?
2. Why us?

When I shared this with Daniel and Elaine, I could see them both thinking back to all the work we'd done on their cover letters and resumes and connecting the dots.

Daniel's "Why you?" answer had always been a laundry list of achievements. Unfortunately, this often backfires, making overqualified candidates seem self-focused or intimidating. Instead, we reframed his answer to lead with potential.

Now when Daniel was asked why he was the best candidate for the role, he planned to say, "Because I bring a proven track record in operations that I'm excited to apply in a company positioned for growth like yours."

Elaine's answer to the "Why us?" question was vague. She'd say things like, "You're an industry leader," but that wasn't a good enough response. To help her stand out, we dug deeper, researching specific projects, leadership philosophies, and community initiatives she could reference. During her next interview, she answered the question by saying, "Because your expansion into renewable energy aligns with both my professional expertise and my personal values."

"Your answers need to connect your skills to their needs and your motivation to their mission," I said. "If either part is missing, you won't stick in their minds."

If you can't answer the "Why you?" and "Why us?" questions with overwhelming clarity, confidence, and evidence, you will not get the job, no matter how many interviews you get or how long you talk.

Here are some things to think about so you can be prepared to answer these two questions in an unforgettable way.

QUESTION #1: WHY YOU?

When a company interviews you, they want to know what makes you different and worth betting on. They're not just looking for someone who can do the job. They're looking for the least risky person who will crush the role, be easy to work with, and stay for years.

"Why you?" doesn't mean "Tell me your greatest hits." It means "Show me that you are low risk and high return." And you don't do that by reciting your resume. You do it by aligning your answers to what they truly care about: potential, agreeableness, retention, and trust. This is something we have already addressed for your resume and LinkedIn profile in Sections 2 and 3 of this book. Now, you just need to do the same thing in the interview. The great news is that you're not starting from scratch.

Still, in interviews, many overqualified candidates revert to answering questions by focusing on qualifications only. Unfortunately, that doesn't prove you'll be the best fit for *this* job, in *this* company, with *this* team. It's like applying to be someone's roommate by listing how many apartments you've lived in. Nobody cares. What they want to know is, will it work between us?

This is where most candidates fall apart. They answer "Why you?" with vague, copy-paste talking points and forget the interviewer has already talked with 50 people this week who've all said the same thing.

In a *Harvard Business Review* article, "How to Answer, 'Why Should We Hire You?' In an Interview," the authors emphasize that interviewers are looking for impact.[30] They recommend crafting a response that focuses on results you've delivered, how you'll solve their current problems, and how you'll adapt to their specific challenges. One key strategy they recommend? Customize your answer to the company's current priorities. Don't just talk about what you did. Explain how you will bring that same impact to the team if you're hired.

But you won't know what they need unless you've done your homework. That's where the second question comes in.

QUESTION #2: WHY US?

This question is the hiring manager's quiet test to determine whether you're actually interested in them, or if they're just another company you applied to on a job board last Tuesday.

"Why us?" is not usually asked so bluntly, but you'll hear it in questions like:

- "What do you know about our company?"
- "Why did you leave your last role?"
- "What kind of teams do you like working with?"
- "What do you do in your free time?"

These questions are indirect ways to measure if you're purposefully seeking out this company, or if you're just desperate for anything that pays.

If you want to win interviews, you have to treat the company like the main character in the story. Their mission. Their values. Their products. Their recent news. Their trajectory. You should know all of it. And you should tie your desire to work there to specific reasons.

Saying, "I'm excited about your growth" isn't enough.

Instead, try, "I saw in your last earnings call that you're investing heavily in AI-driven logistics. I've been researching this space for three years, and I'd love to contribute to that initiative."

That's the kind of answer that passes the test.

In a related *Harvard Business Review* article, "How to Answer, 'Why Do You Want to Work Here?'" the authors argue that you must avoid generalities.[31] Instead, they recommend tying your answer to the company's mission, values, recent developments, and future direction. This doesn't just impress, it removes doubt. It proves you've thought carefully about working there and fitting in, which is exactly what a hiring manager wants.

WHAT IS YOUR UNIQUE SELLING PROPOSITION?

Fitting in is important, but it's not enough, especially if you're seen as overqualified. The real key to getting hired is not just showing you belong; it's showing why you're different in a way that matters to the company. It's answering the question "What is different or unique about this job candidate?"

That's where your unique selling proposition, or USP, comes in.

A USP is a marketing term, but it applies directly to your job search. In business, a USP is the one compelling reason a customer should buy from your company instead of a competitor. It's not a laundry list of everything you can do. It's the specific, distinctive value you provide that others don't.

In the job market, your USP is the one specific combination of skills, experiences, and personal qualities that makes you the best choice for the role. It's the thing that, if removed, would make the company say, "We'd lose something important without them."

Take a look at the Venn diagram in Image 1. One circle represents what the company needs. This is spelled out in the job posting, reinforced in the company's values statement, and confirmed in conversations with current employees. Another circle represents what other candidates do well. This includes all the common skills and experiences you'll be up against. The third circle represents what you do well, including your skills, experience, approach, and perspective. Where your circle overlaps with the company's needs but does *not* overlap with what other candidates do well, that's your USP.

> The real key to getting hired is not just showing you belong; it's showing why you're different in a way that matters to the company.

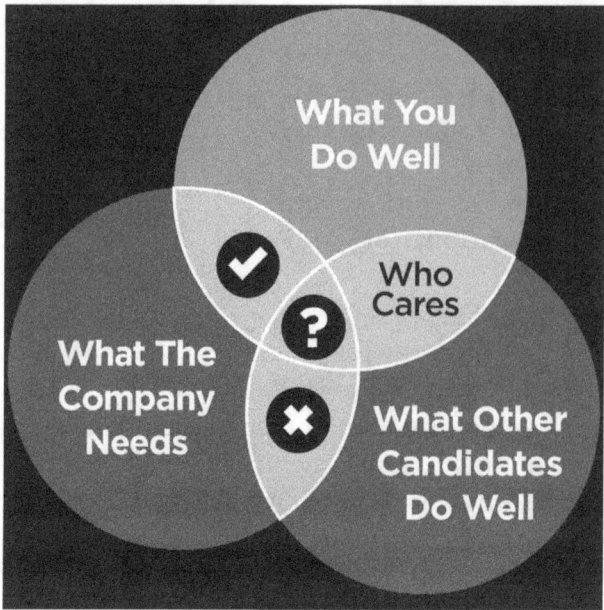

Image 1: The Highly Qualified Candidate's USP

AVOID THE MURKY MIDDLE WHERE EVERY OTHER JOB CANDIDATE LIVES

The danger is in the center of the Venn diagram where all three circles overlap. In the center is where you have what the company needs, what you do well, and what other people do well. That's the space where you blend in. When you're there, you're indistinguishable from everyone else. Your value is murky at best.

If you're indistinguishable from other candidates, hiring managers won't remember you after the interview and you'll become another resume in the pile. The goal is to position yourself in the overlap between your strengths and the company's needs, but outside the overlap with your competitors' strengths.

The mistake most overqualified candidates make is that they compete in the wrong space. They try to prove themselves by showcasing the obvious, extensive leadership experience, deep technical expertise, a long track record of results. The problem is plenty of other candidates have similar claims. This approach often backfires because it can trigger employer concerns about cost, cultural fit, or the fear that you'll leave quickly for something better.

Instead, your USP should shift the conversation from your past accomplishments to your potential to thrive at *their* organization, just like we talked about in Chapters 6 and 7 in Section 1, and then again in Sections 2 and 3, relative to your resume and LinkedIn profile, respectively.

The key is to frame your experience not as a list of historical achievements, but as points of potential and proof that you can solve *their* specific problems, integrate into *their* culture, and contribute over the long-term. It means marketing yourself as a persuasive future solution, not writing an obituary for your career to date.

If you can give them a clear, grounded, and passionate answer for the "Why you?" and "Why us?" questions, proving your unique selling proposition and your deep desire to work there, you will win offers. If you can't, nothing else matters.

So, stop preparing your answers around your background. Start preparing your answers around their goals, culture, and team. Stop worrying about sounding smart. Start worrying about sounding sincere. Stop "playing it cool." Start showing them that you need the job, and not just any job, but this one. And that you want to stay there for the rest of your career.

CHAPTER 31

THE VALUES TEST

"Not only are hiring managers thinking about whether you'll fit in with their team culture; they're watching your body language and listening for your values behind everything you say," I said.

Daniel frowned. "You mean they're judging my opinions?"

"Exactly," I said. "Your behavior and opinions are another signal they can use to determine whether you align with their core values."

"How does what I say reveal my values?" Elaine asked.

"Even a casual question like, 'Tell me about a time you disagreed with a manager,' is a values test," I said. "If you come across as combative, the interviewer might assume you'll be a cultural mismatch. If you seem too passive, they'll doubt your leadership."

"I often answer opinion-based questions by telling it like it is," Elaine said. "Is that wrong?"

"Not wrong," I assured her. "But we can reframe your approach so you can still be authentic but emphasize collaboration, respect, and problem-solving."

"What about me?" Daniel asked.

"You need to balance your confidence with openness using phrases like, 'I see it differently, and here's why, but I'd want to hear other perspectives before deciding,'" I said.

By the end of our session, they understood how to tailor their responses to questions about their behavior and opinions in a way that conveyed their beliefs and still reassured the interviewer that they were the best fit for the role.

BEHAVIORAL QUESTIONS EVALUATE YOUR LEVEL OF PERSONAL RESPONSIBILITY

As I shared in the previous chapters, an interview is less about your resume and more about assessing your personality, behavior, values, and how you respond to stress. If you're an overqualified candidate with decades of experience, multiple degrees, and prior leadership roles, behavioral and opinion-based interview questions are a way for a hiring manager to see if you've stayed grounded or if you've become too abstract, too self-focused, or too removed from how work actually gets done today.

Behavioral questions are almost always rooted in your past. But they're not asking for the past itself, they're asking for your interpretation of it. These questions probe whether you take ownership of your role in the successes and failures of your career.

For example, when asked, "Tell me about a time when you had a conflict on a team," what they really want to know is: do you blame others? Do you criticize or deflect? Or do you own your part, describe how you resolved the situation, and show that you learned from it?

If your answers put all the stress and failure on the team or environment, if you blame your coworkers, call out your manager's poor communication, or complain about toxic culture, you fail the values test. Because no matter how true those details may be, they signal to the interviewer that you don't take responsibility. And responsibility is everything.

Employers are under enormous pressure to avoid hiring anyone who will create problems, stir resentment, or add friction, so they look for red flags in how you frame your past.

If you can't describe a challenge without placing blame or sounding bitter, they will assume you are the problem, even if you weren't.

> Employers are under enormous pressure to avoid hiring anyone who will create problems, stir resentment, or add friction, so they look for red flags in how you frame your past. If you can't describe a challenge without placing blame or sounding bitter, they will assume you are the problem, even if you weren't.

OPINION-BASED QUESTIONS ASSESS YOUR CULTURAL FIT

Opinion-based questions, on the other hand, are forward-facing. With this type of question, an interviewer can present hypothetical scenarios or ask you to express your views on workplace dynamics, success, or leadership.

Although hypothetical, the interviewer is comparing your answer to the company's values. If the company has a *team-first* culture and they ask, "How would you handle an angry customer who's yelling at you?" they want to hear that you'd check in with your team, loop in support, or consult your manager first. If the company has a *customer-first* value, they want to hear that you'd calmly and promptly resolve the issue on your own to protect the relationship. It's the same question, but there's a different right answer depending on the company's value system.

It's not enough to just give smart or experienced-sounding interview answers. You have to speak in alignment with what the company prioritizes. As an overqualified candidate, you're already battling the assumption that you're set in your ways. If your answers show that you haven't adapted to the company's worldview or don't even understand it, that assumption becomes a deal-breaker.

These questions, behavioral and opinion-based, are your chance to show more than experience. They're your chance to show insight, humility, and alignment. They're how you demonstrate that you're not just a person with a long resume, but someone who still knows how to show up, take feedback, listen, adapt, and collaborate.

For candidates with executive backgrounds or long tenure in senior roles, this can be hard. You're used to making decisions, not justifying them. You're used to leading, not explaining. But in interviews today, no matter your past titles, you're being assessed as a peer. A potential team member. And that means showing that you can function, and thrive, under someone else's system, with someone else's priorities.

AN INTERVIEW IS JUST LIKE AN AUDITION

One of the strangest misfires overqualified candidates make during interviews happens at the exact moment they should be securing the job. It's when the conversation turns practical — when an employer asks how you would solve a specific problem, improve a system, or approach a strategic decision.

Instead of leaning in, many candidates recoil. They hesitate. They get cagey. Some say very little. Some act insulted. Others clam up entirely, as if they've just been asked to hand over a proprietary patent or reveal a family secret. The belief is that the company is trying to get something for free. The fear is that their brilliance will be stolen and used without compensation.

Ideas are worthless without capital and execution. You can have the most revolutionary idea in the world, and it won't matter unless the company has the capital, infrastructure, talent, distribution, operations, and support to bring it to life. And unless you're planning to build that infrastructure yourself, you need a job. That's the exchange. When you work for a company, your intellectual property belongs to them. That's what employment contracts say. It's not theft, it's business. And if you don't like the sound of that, you're going to have a hard time getting hired anywhere.

THE VALUES TEST

The companies asking you to solve a problem aren't trying to cheat you. They're testing you. They're offering you a chance to prove your value in real-time. They want to see how you think, how you approach ambiguity, and how you communicate under pressure. Most of all, they want to see if you can externalize your problem-solving process.

> The companies asking you to solve a problem aren't trying to cheat you. They're testing you. They're offering you a chance to prove your value in real-time.

This is not about being a genius. It's about being transparent. It's about walking them through your logic. They're not expecting you to fix their business in a 30-minute interview. They're expecting you to show that you can process a challenge, ask intelligent questions, and propose possible paths forward.

To answer such questions, start by recapping what you've just been asked. Literally say, "So what I'm hearing is you're facing [Problem 1], [Problem 2], and [Problem 3], and you're trying to get to [Outcome 1], is that right?" That alone shows alignment. It shows you're listening.

Then, start building scenarios.

Don't say, "I'd just do this." That sounds rigid.

Instead, say, "I'd start by meeting with key stakeholders, whoever owns [Problem 1], [Problem 2], and [Problem 3], and reviewing any existing data. Based on that, if we saw these early indicators, I might explore this route. But if the data leaned more toward [Outcome 1], we'd need to go in a different direction. And if it turned out [Outcome 2] was the main constraint, then I'd look at these additional options."

In other words, open the door to possibility. Be flexible. Be thoughtful. Show that you're not just full of ideas, you're capable of refining those ideas with input and collaboration. That's what they care about.

PRACTICE MIRRORING VALUE AND EXPRESSING PERSONAL OWNERSHIP

Before your next interview, prepare answers to behavioral questions that show ownership, not blame. Describe situations where you made mistakes, fixed them, and learned. Show them you're a fountainhead of ideas. Share examples of collaboration, conflict resolution, and problem-solving that end with team success, not just personal achievement. Then, when it comes to opinion-based questions, do your research. Study the company's values, listen to their leaders, review their mission statements and marketing language. Align your responses accordingly.

Remember to speak their language too. If their mission is innovation, show how you've embraced change. If it's teamwork, describe a time you deferred to others for the good of the group. If it's service, tell a story about putting someone else's needs first. Every word you say is being measured against the company's culture, and whether or not you're able to take responsibility for yourself.

CHAPTER 32

WORK SAMPLES AND ASSESSMENTS

Daniel had recently been asked to complete a timed case study for a job he wanted. "I didn't think it was fair," he told me. "They should know I can do the work based on my resume."

I shook my head. "In today's market, assessments and work samples are the new normal. The good news is, they're your chance to show, not just tell, what you can do for the company."

Elaine remembered once declining an unpaid project request. "I didn't want to give away free work," she said.

"There's a difference between exploitation and strategic proof. A relevant, manageable work sample can set you apart — especially if you're overqualified and they're looking for reassurance you'll be hands-on," I said.

I recalled helping a client years ago who landed an executive role after building a one-page mock plan for her first 90 days. "It wasn't about free labor," I told Daniel and Elaine. "It was about eliminating doubt."

To make sure they'd always be prepared to share a work sample if requested, we spent some time building small portfolios with select, short samples that could be customized for different roles. "If you want the job," I said, "show them the quality of your work before they even ask."

YOUR LICENSE TO PROVE WHAT YOU'VE ACCOMPLISHED

Unlike all the previous chapters of this book, where I've told you that potential is more important than proof, this part of the job search process is your opportunity to show what you've accomplished. The difference now is that you're proving what you've done and what you're capable of with samples and test answers, not just what you say about yourself on a resume or online profile.

Take a moment and think about hiring from the employer's point of view: they're expected to select someone who will be embedded in their team, handed access to confidential information, trusted with customer relationships, and paid a significant salary, all based on what that person chose to include in a resume and how they act during two or three hours of curated interaction. If you had to choose a business partner or roommate that way, would you? Probably not.

This is why job candidates are increasingly being asked to complete assessments, submit work samples, and even perform trial tasks before they can advance in the hiring process. This shift will only accelerate with the rise of AI tools that make these evaluations easier, faster, and more predictive. If you're not prepared for this, you're not ready to be hired.

FROM SUBTLE AI SIGNALS TO REAL-TIME BEHAVIORAL TEST QUESTIONS

I previously shared about how machine learning systems use linguistic cues and behavioral markers to predict whether a candidate will stay at a company for two years or more using frameworks like the Big Five. Now, those same principles are being applied in the hiring process in the form of applicant assessments.

You may be asked to take a behavioral test, complete a time-limited problem-solving task, or submit a detailed portfolio of past work. You may even be asked to record yourself responding to questions on video or to build a prototype. Don't take these requests personally; they're not trying to get free labor from you. They're trying to de-risk a decision that could cost them tens of thousands of dollars if they get it wrong.

If you've read this far in the book, you already know the deeper truth: your resume and past experience are the least predictive signals of your long-term success. It's how you think, act, and solve problems that matters. These assessments are your opportunity to prove that.

COLLECT DELIVERABLES AND CREATE A DIGITAL PORTFOLIO BEFORE YOU NEED IT

The reason companies are investing so heavily in these assessment layers is not just that they want better hires; it's because technology now allows them to do it with very little effort. Behavioral tests, work simulations, portfolio reviews, and even AI-generated interview analysis can all be run with just a few clicks. It costs them nothing compared to the cost of turnover. They can set it up once and run thousands of candidates through it automatically. There's no reason they won't keep doing it, and every reason they will.

Expect the number and intensity of these evaluations to increase over the coming years. But don't be intimidated. This is not a bad thing for you. For a truly overqualified candidate, someone with depth, adaptability, and clarity, this is a huge opportunity to stand out. You no longer have to rely on a two-page resume to explain who you are. You can show it. And the employers who are worth working for will appreciate that.

The best strategy you can adopt is to build a digital portfolio right now, before you're asked for one. It doesn't matter what field you're in. You can collect deliverables, reports, designs, slide decks, product outlines, process documentation, sales scripts, customer journeys, training materials, whatever represents your work. If you can't use real examples because of nondisclosure agreements or proprietary data, then recreate them with fictitious details.

The format doesn't matter; what matters is that you can demonstrate how you think and what you've done. Store these in a cloud-based folder and create a shareable link. Then put that link on your resume. This single step will make you stand out more than any buzzword or summary statement ever could. It shows initiative, transparency, and a willingness to engage with the hiring process more seriously than 95% of candidates.

CHAPTER 33

IF YOUR WI-FI DROPS, SO DO YOU: MASTERING TECH TO GET HIRED

Elaine laughed when I told her that a video interview could be lost over a bad connection. "Surely they'd reschedule?"

We were five weeks into our work together, and I was describing how even the smallest tech issues, both visual and audio, affect hiring today.

"Not always," I said. "Tech issues in interviews can knock you out, especially when there are plenty of other candidates."

Daniel had been late to a virtual interview once because his platform wouldn't load. That was enough for the employer to move on. "It's not fair," he said.

"It's about perception, not fairness," I replied. "If you can't manage tech in the interview, they'll assume you can't in the job."

To help Daniel and Elaine avoid any future tech issues, I taught them my four-step, pre-interview checklist:

1. Test equipment the day before.
2. Have a backup device ready.

3. Know how to switch to phone audio.
4. Keep contact info handy.

Then, we practiced looking directly into the camera, lighting their faces well, and framing themselves at eye level so they could show up professionally in a virtual setting.

If your Wi-Fi drops during a job interview, you drop from their list of candidates. That's the reality of today's hiring process. A hardline connection is no longer a nice-to-have; it's the baseline. Employers have zero tolerance for candidates who fail on basic technology. You can have all the experience in the world, but if your video glitches, your audio is fuzzy, or your camera angle looks like you're filming a horror movie from under your desk, you're done.

Employers aren't going to say it, but they will disqualify you without hesitation. Why? Because today's workplace is hybrid at best and remote at scale. Yes, they're hiring you for your expertise and culture fit, but they're also hiring your ability to function on tech platforms from day one without needing to be babysat.

THE TECH ESSENTIALS YOU NEED FOR SUCCESS

Let's start with the essentials. Your first step is to get a wired internet connection. If your laptop doesn't have an Ethernet port, buy an adapter. If your router is on the other side of the house, run a cable to your computer or move your setup. If you're serious about getting hired, show it.

Lighting also matters and so does audio. Bad audio is a deal-breaker. Most studies show that viewers will tolerate poor video before they tolerate poor sound. To solve a poor audio problem, get an external microphone — not your laptop mic, not your AirPods, an actual external mic. You can get one for $20 to $40. Same with lighting. Set up a few lamps if you have to, but ideally, buy a basic lighting kit.

Even your background matters now. A messy room, a cluttered bookcase, even a weird shadow behind you, these things signal a lack of self-awareness. If you want to appear professional in a virtual interview, set yourself up in front of a blank wall. Ideally, buy a green sheet online for less than $10 and use a clean, high-resolution virtual background.

Your camera should be positioned directly at eye level, not pointed up your nose or showing only the top of your head. Frame yourself like a newscaster so that the top of your head to the middle of your torso are in the shot.

Finally, test the video software *before* the interview. Don't log in two minutes before start time and find out that Zoom needs an update or your mic isn't recognized. That's amateur hour, and you will be remembered for it, but not in a good way.

Don't make the mistake of thinking the quality of your audio, video, lighting, and background doesn't apply to you because of your past title or years of experience. In fact, if you were a Senior Vice President or a CEO before, these elements will be *more* critical for your success (or failure) in an interview. Hiring managers will assume you're out of touch, or worse, that you think you're above it all. This is a landmine for anyone over 40, especially if you haven't interviewed in the last five years.

AI VIDEO INTERVIEWS ARE ALREADY HERE

Today's interview expectations include a virtual baseline that was optional five years ago. Video resumes are on the rise. So are one-way recorded interviews, where you answer preloaded questions. These trends may not be widespread yet, but they are gaining traction. If you freeze or fumble through your elevator pitch on video, that's the only thing the AI system analyzing your submission will see.

Current AI interview tools measure things like speech cadence, tone, energy, word choice, and microexpressions. A recent study published in the *Social Science Research Network* journal, "AI Personality Extraction from Faces: Labor Market Implications," found that new AI models can predict a job candidate's Big Five personality profile and career success from a single image of their face.[32]

Whether or not you like it, new AI tools are being used to screen out candidates visually now too. But don't get discouraged. These tools look for consistency and effort, even by video. That's why your lighting, sound, posture, and energy levels all matter. Smile. Sit up straight. Keep your energy up. If you let your face droop, you look bored or disengaged. If your eyes dart around or you're clearly reading from a script, the system catches that too. Treat it like a performance because that's exactly what it is.

THE VIRTUAL TEST AND THE IN-PERSON TEST

The irony is that while screening is becoming more technologically advanced, hiring still ends with a human. More often than not, you will be invited to an in-person interview after passing through the virtual gates. That means you need to master both digital and physical presence. You need to know how to give a firm handshake, maintain eye contact, and make small talk with people younger, older, and from all walks of life.

Employers want to see that you still know how to be human in a professional setting. If you've been unemployed for a while or working remotely alone for too long, this matters more than you think.

Don't assume your in-person skills are still sharp just because they were five years ago. Practice them. Go to networking events. Have live conversations. Sit down with someone and get comfortable holding their gaze, modulating your voice, and keeping your energy consistent for hours. Site visits are still part of the interview process, especially for high-level roles, so think about whether you can keep your energy high through eight hours of meetings.

In this new age of hiring, it's not enough to look good on paper. You have to look good on screen and in person too. You have to be both technically competent and emotionally intelligent. You have to understand how to navigate a world where AI might be your first interviewer, but a human will still have the final say in whether you're hired or not. If you're not willing to evolve, you will be left behind.

CHAPTER 34

LEVERAGE INTERVIEWS TO CLOSE THE DEAL

Daniel had been treating interviews like final exams. He'd answer every question and hope for a passing grade. When he shared this with me, I said, "You're not a student; you're a business negotiating a deal."

"I think I understand what you're saying," Elaine said. "But what does that mean in practice?"

"It means you should be evaluating the employer as much as they're evaluating you," I said. "If you have options, you have leverage."

Many of my clients over the years had lost offers by putting all their hopes into a single opportunity, so I knew Daniel and Elaine needed to learn to cultivate their options, keep multiple processes moving, network while interviewing, and never stop outreach after one good interview.

"If you have another option in play, you could negotiate or walk away from a position that's not the best fit," I said. "But you can only do that if you learn how to navigate the late-stage-interview phase of the hiring process."

By reframing interviews as mutual evaluations, Daniel and Elaine started asking better questions, signaling confidence, and subtly reminding employers they had other opportunities.

"Options aren't arrogance," I told them. "They're insurance."

Too many job seekers treat their first sign of traction like the finish line instead of the starting gun. They finally get a recruiter to call them back, land a phone screening, or move to the first round of interviews, and their immediate instinct is to shut down all other job search activity. They stop networking, applying, and following up with other leads.

They think, *I've got something going here, time to focus on this one.* It's an understandable reaction — especially if the job search has been slow or exhausting — but it's one of the biggest mistakes you can make because when your one lead stalls, or disappears entirely, you're back at square one. The other opportunities you put on hold have gone cold, and you have to rebuild momentum from scratch. That lag in activity not only kills your pipeline but also kills your leverage. And leverage is everything.

GETTING HIRED IS A DEAL-MAKING PROCESS, NOT A MORAL EVALUATION OF WORTH

Think of today's job market as an exchange of value between two parties. Employers have something you want: a job, salary, benefits, a career path. You have something they want: skills, experience, cultural alignment, potential. A deal is made when both parties believe they're getting more value than they're giving up.

If you're getting low-quality job offers, that's not a sign that you're worth less. It's a sign that you're not communicating

> **If you're getting low-quality job offers, that's not a sign that you're worth less. It's a sign that you're not communicating value in the way the employer sees it.**

value in the way the employer sees it. You may think your value is in your years of experience or the complexity of your past work, but the employer might define value as someone who is agreeable, easy to manage, willing to take direction, adaptable, and able to solve problems without creating new ones. Value is in the eye of the beholder. You have to position yourself as someone who can deliver more than what's in the job description, and who can do it in a way that makes the hiring manager's life easier.

Every time something positive happens in your job search, whether it's an interview request, a second-round invitation, or even a recruiter asking for more information, you should treat it like a signal flare. Once that happens, you can go to every other contact, recruiter, and hiring manager you've been talking to and let them know you're in demand. Tell them you have an interview lined up, but their company is your top choice because of specific reasons tied to their role, culture, or mission. Ask if you can move your conversation forward before you have to decide elsewhere.

If this feels dishonest, remember that you can have multiple top choices for different reasons. One company might be your top choice for culture, another for location, and another for career growth. What matters is that you communicate genuine interest while signaling that others are also pursuing you. This social proof makes you seem more desirable because it's human nature to want what other people want or have.

And, like all negotiations, the party that's less emotionally attached to the outcome has more power. Having multiple active opportunities naturally makes you care less about any one of them, which in turn makes you a stronger negotiator. You can walk away if the terms aren't right. You can push for more because you have alternatives. You don't need to bluff; you just need to keep creating options.

CONSTANTLY FEED YOUR PIPELINE, EVEN WHEN YOU'RE IN LATE-STAGE INTERVIEWS

It's tempting to conserve energy and focus only on the opportunity that's in front of you, but that's lazy thinking disguised as strategy. Most interviews don't result in offers, and now that technology enables employers to screen dozens of candidates quickly, the odds of making it through without competition are slim. So instead of slowing down when you get traction, you need to accelerate.

If you want to continue creating options for yourself so you can have real leverage during the deal-making (hiring) process, you should use each sign of interest to pry open doors that were previously closed. Reach back out to people who ghosted you. Contact recruiters who haven't responded in weeks. Say things like, "I'm in conversations with another company now, but your company is my first choice for [specific reason]. Could we set up a time to talk before I have to decide?" That social proof is believable and creates urgency.

START THINKING ABOUT GETTING HIRED LIKE AN EXCHANGE OF VALUE

Once you see the job search as a deal-making process, your approach changes. When you have multiple companies interested in you, you have the power to decide which deal is best instead of feeling like you need to accept the first position offered. You stop thinking, *Am I good enough for them?* and start thinking, *Is this a mutually beneficial exchange of value?* That mental shift alone will make you more confident, more selective, and more persuasive.

This mindset also sets you up perfectly for salary negotiation. If you've been building leverage through multiple options, you can negotiate from a position of strength. You're not forced to accept the first number they throw at you because you have other offers, or the real possibility of other offers, on the table. You can say, "I'm excited about this opportunity, but I do have other companies interested. If we can get to [desired salary], I'd be happy to move forward with you."

And having other options doesn't just give you leverage on compensation. It gives you leverage on start dates, benefits, role responsibilities, and career path discussions. It turns you from a passive recipient of whatever an employer offers into an active participant in shaping the deal.

Remember that in a job search, options are leverage. And leverage is the bridge between interviewing and negotiating. The more you have, the better your deals will be. The mistake is thinking you can coast into a single opportunity and win. The reality is you have to keep creating opportunities until the ink is dry on an offer letter you actually want to sign.

CHAPTER 35

HOW TO WIN THE SALARY NEGOTIATION

At the end of the week Elaine finally got an offer. She joined our meeting excited, but I could see that she was also anxious. "How do I make sure I don't leave money on the table?" she asked.

I smiled. "I'm so glad you asked," I said. "The first thing you need to do is deflect until the company puts out the first number. When they do, you'll want to use precise figures rather than round ones to work toward an agreement. You should also avoid muddying the waters by mixing variables and instead, negotiate base salary first, then signing bonus, relocation, incentives, equity, and vacation."

"Wow, there's more to a salary than a little back-and-forth," Elaine said.

"But won't pushing back on salary potentially ruin my chance to truly close the deal? What if the employer doesn't like that?" Daniel asked.

"This isn't about greed," I told them. "It's about valuing yourself and signaling that you know the market. Employers respect candidates who negotiate well."

To make sure Elaine and Daniel were prepared to negotiate for the salaries they wanted, we practiced asking open-ended questions like, "How flexible can we be on total compensation?" rather than making ultimatums. We also practiced negotiating in the right order to prevent one category of compensation from cannibalizing another. By the end of our sessions, both could walk into a negotiation confident, calm, and prepared.

LEVERAGE IS THE CURRENCY OF NEGOTIATION

Most job seekers see negotiation as the final act of their job search. They imagine it happening only after a long process of screening calls, video interviews, a final in-person meeting, and the reference checks. Only when the employer slides the offer across the table does the word "negotiation" even cross their mind. This is a costly mistake.

Negotiation starts immediately after the first phone screen, the referral conversation, or a recruiter's initial outreach. All of these interactions shape how the company values you. From the moment you first make contact, you are in an unspoken exchange of value. If you fail to realize this, you'll be negotiating from a position of weakness before the real conversation even begins.

So, how do you win the salary negotiation process?

In the current job market, the biggest negotiation risk isn't getting a low offer; it's never having the leverage to move the offer at all. Employers are under no obligation to start a negotiation with a high offer, and they expect candidates to counter. In fact, if you accept the first offer without hesitation, you can actually trigger suspicion. They may wonder if you undervalue yourself, or worse, if you're not truly competitive in the market.

Accepting the first offer without countering can flatten your career trajectory for decades. The starting salary you agree to today becomes the foundation for all future earnings, even at other companies, because most employers use past salary as an anchor in determining new offers.

Too many job seekers make the fatal error of narrowing their search as soon as one opportunity starts moving forward. They drop their other applications, slow their networking, and put all their hopes on the one process. When it falls through, as it often does, they're forced to start over. The smarter play is to turn every bit of positive progress into a bargaining chip as discussed in Chapter 34.

When the salary discussion begins in earnest, the first rule is simple: never name the first number. Whether it's a field on a job application asking for your desired salary or a recruiter pressing for your expectations in the first call, deflect. Early in the process, you don't have enough information to set a number and giving one can get you screened out before you ever explain your value.

Online applications can be especially dangerous because AI systems can filter out candidates whose number is even slightly above an internal threshold. If you must enter a figure, consider providing a range that starts 10–20% lower than the listed range or your market research suggests, then negotiate upward later by saying, "Now that I've learned more about the role and responsibilities, I'd like to revisit the numbers."

EXPAND YOUR OPTIONS FOR A BETTER DEAL BY ASKING OPEN-ENDED QUESTIONS

Once an offer is on the table, think of it as a conditional offer, not a final one. Your first response should be gratitude paired with an open-ended question:

"Thank you for the offer, I really appreciate it. I believe I can bring [specific value] to the company, but the numbers don't look quite right. What can we do to increase the salary?"

This invites collaboration, avoids yes/no dead-ends, and keeps you positioned as a team player.

Open-ended negotiation questions can also create unexpected movement. Asking, "Is this the best you can do?" challenges the employer to find an additional budget. "What skills or experiences would put me at the top of the salary range for this role?" invites them to justify paying you more. "How did you calculate this offer?" can open a revealing discussion about internal pay bands and budget flexibility.

Another powerful strategy is negotiating in sequence, not all at once. Address base salary first, because other components like signing bonus, incentives, relocation assistance, equity, and extra vacation are easier to move once salary is set. Bundling all of these elements too early can lead to trade-offs that don't serve you. When it comes to numbers, precision is your ally.

PRECISE NUMBERS HELP YOU INCREASE THEIR FINAL OFFER

In an analysis of nearly 2,000 corporate acquisition offers over three decades, Petri Hukkanen of Boston Consulting Group found that "round initial offers were less likely to secure a deal than precise offers" and, when deals did close, the rounded offers "ended up costing the bidder more."[33] The market reaction to precise offers was also 2% higher, signaling greater confidence.

In other words, $131,500 sounds calculated and defensible. On the other hand, $130,000 sounds arbitrary.

Precision projects authority, suggests you've done detailed research, and can even create doubt in the other side's assumptions, tilting the conversation in your favor. Still, precision should be used with judgment. Don't cross into absurdity with hyper-specific figures like $157,252.25, which can appear inauthentic or rigid. Instead, aim for numbers that are exact enough to imply calculation but reasonable enough to keep the discussion fluid. This balance reinforces your credibility and maintains rapport, both essential to a positive negotiation outcome.

BECOME A SUCCESSFUL NEGOTIATOR

It's important not to forget that recruiters and hiring managers do not work for you. They work for the company. Any negotiation advice they give you serves their goal of securing talent at the best price for their employer. This fact doesn't make them adversaries, but it does mean you should treat their guidance with critical evaluation as you would any party on the other side of a deal. Instead, seek advice from people whose interests are aligned with yours, such as trusted peers or mentors, and test every recommendation against your own research and objectives.

Negotiation is not a one-off event; it's a skill you refine over time. Each conversation is a chance to practice deflection, precision, sequencing, and open-ended questioning. The most successful negotiators approach it as an ongoing dialogue, not a battle to be won in a single exchange. They understand that compensation is a package, not a number, and they know that perceived value — what the employer believes they are getting — matters far more than actual qualifications in determining pay. They don't just ask for more; they show why they're worth more in terms that the employer cares about: being agreeable, dependable, adaptable, and able to deliver results beyond the stated role.

The difference between someone who accepts the first offer and someone who negotiates with skill is often measured in hundreds of thousands, sometimes millions, over a career. The starting salary you secure today can compound for decades. And the leverage you build by keeping your options open doesn't just help you land the job; it ensures you get paid what you're truly worth once you do.

CHAPTER 36

IT ONLY TAKES ONE YES TO CHANGE EVERYTHING

I told Daniel and Elaine what I tell every client: "It only takes one yes. And that yes is still out there."

Daniel's yes came first — a mid-sized firm that valued his operational expertise and collaborative mindset. Elaine's followed two weeks later at a company that needed her bridge-building skills during a major expansion. Her first offer had fallen through, but this one was better anyway, and the company was a better fit.

As we celebrated, I said, "You didn't get here by luck. You got here by shifting your approach and being mentally tough, leading with potential, showing agreeableness, targeting your resume, building relationships, and staying in the game."

I thought of my parents and how things might have been different if they'd had this knowledge when the job market turned against them. Daniel and Elaine's success was a reminder of why I do this work. I've seen what's at stake and know that a job is often the cornerstone of security, dignity, and even family stability.

Before Daniel and Elaine left our final meeting, I said, "Keep applying what you've learned. Stay adaptable. Keep reaching out. This isn't the end; it's the start of a stronger chapter in your career."

YOUR YES IS STILL OUT THERE

There's a moment in every job search when the noise gets so loud you start to believe that your experience is too much, that your skills are somehow outdated, or that the market has passed you by. You start to believe the good opportunities are gone, or that they belong to someone younger, cheaper, or with a different kind of background.

That's the point when you must stop, take a breath, and remember that it only takes one yes. One yes to put you in the right role for your life right now. One yes to turn months or years of frustration into momentum. One yes to make all the rejections fade into the background.

The scope of opportunity is bigger than it feels from inside your search. There are more than 33 million companies in the United States alone. Every single one of them needs help. Many need it urgently. Jobs exist in every size and shape in roles you've heard of, roles you haven't, and roles that are being created right now because a problem emerged this morning that someone has to solve.

The person who wins in this market is not the one with the perfect resume or the most flawless interview answers. It's the one who stays in the game long enough to find the right match. The one who understands that a "no" is just a data point, not a verdict. The one who sees every conversation as a bridge to the next opportunity, and every rejection as proof they're still active in the market.

Your power lies in the next introduction, next message, next coffee meeting, next application, and next follow-up. This mindset turns the search from a series of dead-ends into a series of steppingstones. You can't control when the yes comes, but you can control how many opportunities you put yourself in front of until it does.

MENTAL STRENGTH IS WHAT KEEPS YOU MOVING WHEN IT FEELS POINTLESS

Searching for a job when you're at or near the peak of your career, or after you've spent decades building expertise, can feel like a betrayal when the market doesn't instantly recognize your value. That feeling can turn into bitterness if you let it, and bitterness repels opportunity.

Mental strength is what helps you keep making calls, sending messages, and showing up at events after weeks or months of silence. It's what allows you to approach each new opportunity fresh, without letting the weight of past rejections drag your energy down. This is not false optimism; it's strategic endurance. Employers are drawn to people who see possibilities and bring energy, even after setbacks.

When you internalize that it only takes one yes, the math of rejection changes. If you get 100 rejections, the 101st conversation could be the one that opens the door. If you've been passed over for a dozen roles you were perfect for, the next one could be the role that sees not just your resume but your full value. You don't need every employer to agree; you just need the right one to say yes at the right time. And that's not luck. That's the direct result of persistence, visibility, and knowing where the real opportunities live.

Someone is getting hired today who has less experience than you, fewer results than you, and less to offer than you. They got the yes because they were in the right place at the right time, and they kept showing up until the timing aligned. That can be you, if you keep showing up.

There is no expiration date on your value. There is no point at which the entire job market agrees you're done. There is only the question of whether you will stay in motion long enough to connect with the role that's right for you right now.

Everything we've discussed — showing commitment, aligning for culture, leading with potential, being agreeable, positioning yourself as a solution, and knowing your worth — has been about giving you the tools to reach that one yes. When you strip away the noise, the strategies, and even the numbers, the heart of the job search is this: you are looking for a single agreement that changes the direction of your life. That agreement exists. The employer who needs you exists. Your only job is to keep going until you find each other.

APPLY WHAT YOU'VE LEARNED IN THIS BOOK, AND YOU WILL GET HIRED

Show employers your value in terms they understand. Be agreeable, because people hire people they want to work with. Build relationships before you need them. Step off the public job boards and into the hidden market where most real opportunities live. Control your narrative instead of letting others define it. Lead with your unique selling proposition, the one thing that makes you the obvious choice.

Be strategic in every conversation, from the first coffee meeting to the final salary negotiation. Deflect until you have leverage, then negotiate in the right order and with precise numbers that communicate authority. Don't round your value down, ever. Recognize that AI, ATS systems, and gatekeepers are designed to screen you out, so position yourself to bypass them through networking, referrals, and tailored messaging. Update your resume to a functional or hybrid format. Adapt your LinkedIn profile to increase your SSI score. Polish your online behavior. Prevent the systems that are reading your digital footprint and profiling you from discounting you. Protect your mental energy and stay in motion, because the person who keeps moving is the one who connects with opportunity.

You've read 36 chapters worth of strategies, now put them to work. The market is big enough for you. The right role is out there for you. And the moment you get that one yes, everything changes.

CHAPTER 37

START MAKING THE 2MM SHIFTS THAT GET YOU HIRED

If you've read this far, you know the job market isn't a gentle place right now. It's more like a fight you didn't ask for but have to win anyway.

The first truth you have to accept is that the job search will be brutal. Not unfair, not rigged, brutal. If you go into this experience expecting the phone to light up with calls from eager employers, you're going to get blindsided. In order to soften the blow and pave a clearer path to your next role, getting help from a career consultant who understands exactly what job candidates like you face in today's market is one of the best things you can do to increase your chances of success.

Most overqualified job candidates think needing help with their job search is a sign of weakness. It isn't. It's a sign that the system has changed faster than you have been told and that you're smart enough to realize it.

The truth is, at this level, you can't crank the engine by yourself anymore. Years ago, you could fix your own car with a wrench and a little persistence. Today, even a simple repair requires a certified technician with diagnostic software to access a vehicle packed with over a hundred computers. The current job market works the same way. Artificial intelligence, behavioral algorithms, reputation scores, and machine learning filters have replaced human gatekeepers. You're not broken; the engine is just more complex, and you need a mechanic who knows how it works.

Though most overqualified professionals aren't lacking effort, what holds them back is the months or even years they lose to trial and error. They keep applying, tweaking their resumes, rewriting cover letters, and waiting for results that never come. They tell themselves it's just bad luck, but really, it's blind spots. You don't know what you don't know. How AI scores your digital footprint, how your resume is profiled for the Big Five personality traits, and how your LinkedIn activity feeds into hidden ranking systems that influence every hiring decision are not things you can figure out by guessing. And every day spent guessing has a cost.

Let's break this down with some simple math. At a $120K salary, each month out of work costs you $10K in opportunity cost. Multiply that by six months, and you've already paid $60K trying to understand and navigate the current job market alone.

You wouldn't let your car sit in the driveway for half a year because you didn't want to call a mechanic, would you? No. You'd get help because you know time is money. The same is true here. Getting expert help isn't indulgence. It's efficiency.

It doesn't take a superhuman effort to get hired again. It takes precision. A small, deliberate 2 mm shift in your approach, compounded over time. Fifteen focused minutes a day applied to the right actions — targeting, outreach, negotiation — will move you miles closer to your next role than months of random effort. But you have to know where to apply those minutes. That's where guidance matters most.

That's why I do this work.

For nearly two decades, I've helped more than 20,000 professionals who were labeled "overqualified" get rehired. People like Daniel and Elaine, who felt invisible until they learned how to re-enter a system that had quietly locked them out. With the right strategy, they didn't just get jobs. They got leverage, dignity, and momentum again.

You can do the same. You've spent your career solving problems for everyone else. Now it's time to solve the problem that stands between you and your next chapter: how to make the market see you again. You don't need to do it alone. The smartest thing you can do is work with someone who knows how the engine runs, who can help you make those 2 mm shifts that turn stalled potential into movement.

You've come this far because you're capable. Now it's time to be strategic.

Get help. Get focused. Get hired.

The system is complex, but it's still navigable. And as I've told every client who's sat across from me, it only takes one yes to change everything.

Get your yes, and a free companion *Too Good to Get Hired Workbook*, at TooGoodGift.com.

ENDNOTES

1. Roman V. Galperin et al., "Too Good to Hire? Capability and Inferences about Commitment in Labor Markets," *Administrative Science Quarterly* 65, no. 2 (March 28, 2019): 275–313, https://doi.org/10.1177/0001839219840022.
2. "Cost of Living Has Risen 20% since 2021 - so Why Are Inflation Rates so Low?," *Yahoo! Finance*, accessed November 4, 2025, https://finance.yahoo.com/news/cost-living-risen-20-since-120032329.html; Hiranmayi Srinivasan, "Historical U.S. Inflation Rate by Year: 1929 to 2025," *Investopedia*, accessed November 4, 2025, https://www.investopedia.com/inflation-rate-by-year-7253832#.
3. Shan P Tsai et al., "Age at Retirement and Long Term Survival of an Industrial Population: Prospective Cohort Study," *BMJ* 331, no. 7523 (October 21, 2005): 995, https://doi.org/10.1136/bmj.38586.448704.e0.
4. Chenkai Wu et al., "Association of Retirement Age with Mortality: A Population-Based Longitudinal Study among Older Adults in the USA," *Journal of Epidemiology and Community Health* 70, no. 9 (March 21, 2016): 917–23, https://doi.org/10.1136/jech-2015-207097.
5. Heidi Grant, "The Surprising Secret to Selling Yourself," *Harvard Business Review*, August 29, 2012, https://hbr.org/2012/08/the-surprising-secret-to-selli.
6. Zakary L. Tormala, Jayson S. Jia, and Michael I. Norton, "The Preference for Potential," *Journal of Personality and Social Psychology* 103, no. 4 (October 2012): 567–83, https://doi.org/10.1037/a0029227.

7   Ginger Christ, "Companies Tend to Hire Based on Vibes, Not Skills, Study Shows," *HR Dive*, April 29, 2025, https://www.hrdive.com/news/companies-tend-to-hire-based-on-vibes-not-skills/746596/.
8   Michael P. Wilmot and Deniz S Ones, "Agreeableness and Its Consequences: A Quantitative Review of Meta-Analytic Findings," *Academy of Management Proceedings* 2022, no. 1 (August 2022), https://doi.org/10.5465/ambpp.2022.10171abstract.
9   Soo Ling Lim et al., "Kill Chaos with Kindness: Agreeableness Improves Team Performance under Uncertainty," *Collective Intelligence* 2, no. 1 (January 2023), https://doi.org/10.1177/26339137231158584.
10 Osama Alhendi, "Personality Traits and Their Validity in Predicting Job Performance at Recruitment: A Review," *International Journal of Engineering and Management Sciences* 4, no. 3 (September 9, 2019): 222–31, https://doi.org/10.21791/ijems.2019.3.21.
11 Mimi Aboubaker, "Finding a Job When You Don't Know What You Want to Do Next," *Harvard Business Review*, January 28, 2022, https://hbr.org/2022/01/finding-a-job-when-you-dont-know-what-you-want-to-do-next.
12 Lindsay Ellis, "You're Fighting AI with AI: Bots Are Breaking the Hiring Process," *Wall Street Journal*, May 10, 2024, https://www.wsj.com/lifestyle/careers/ai-job-application-685f29f7.
13 "3 in 10 Companies Currently Have Fake Job Postings Listed - ResumeBuilder.com," *ResumeBuilder.com*, 18 July 2024, www.resumebuilder.com/3-in-10-companies-currently-have-fake-job-posting-listed/; "That Job You Applied for Might Not Exist. Here's What's behind a Boom in 'Ghost Jobs,'" *CBS News*, accessed November 5, 2025, https://www.cbsnews.com/news/fake-job-listing-ghost-jobs-cbs-news-explains/.
14 Kailyn Rhone, "Does Your Résumé Pass the Six-Second Test?" *Wall Street Journal*, April 16, 2023, https://www.wsj.com/tech/does-your-resume-pass-the-six-second-test-b63f4c02.

15 ABC News, accessed November 6, 2025, https://abcnews.go.com/Business/recipe-perfect-resume-revealed/story?id=23782664; "Keeping an eye on recruiter behavior," accessed November 6, 2025, https://www.bu.edu/com/files/2018/10/TheLadders-EyeTracking-StudyC2.pdf.
16 Camille Cunningham, "What Is Keyphrase Density and Why Is It Important?," *Yoast*, November 4, 2025, https://yoast.com/what-is-keyphrase-density-and-why-is-it-important/.
17 Sébastien Fernandez et al., "Using Available Signals on LinkedIn for Personality Assessment," *Journal of Research in Personality* 93 (August 2021): 104122, https://doi.org/10.1016/j.jrp.2021.104122.
18 Eric Grunenberg et al., "Machine learning in recruiting: predicting personality from CVS and short text responses," *Frontiers in Social Psychology* 1 (January 29, 2024), https://doi.org/10.3389/frsps.2023.1290295.
19 "Your forgotten digital footprints could hurt your job prospects. Here's how to act now," *Fast Company*, accessed November 7, 2025, https://www.fastcompany.com/90776360/your-forgotten-digital-footprints-could-hurt-your-job-prospects-heres-how-to-act-now; Niall McCarthy and Felix Richter, "Infographic: Study: A Comprehensive LinkedIn Profile Boosts Job Chances," *Statista Daily Data*, April 1, 2019, https://www.statista.com/chart/17535/linkedin-profile-boosts-job-chances.
20 "White Paper: Linguistic Fingerprinting to Flag AI Authorship Cheating," *FLINT AI*, March 4, 2023, https://flintai.com/white-paper.php.
21 Karthik Rajkumar et al., "A Causal Test of the Strength of Weak Ties," *Science* 377, no. 6612 (September 16, 2022): 1304–10, https://doi.org/10.1126/science.abl4476.
22 Ilana Gershon, "'A Friend of a Friend' Is No Longer the Best Way to Find a Job," *Harvard Business Review*, June 2, 2017, https://hbr.org/2017/06/a-friend-of-a-friend-is-no-longer-the-best-way-to-find-a-job.
23 Alison Wood Brooks and Leslie K. John, "The Surprising Power of Questions," *Harvard Business Review*, May 1, 2018, https://hbr.org/2018/05/the-surprising-power-of-questions.

24. Armin Falk and Urs Fischbacher, "A Theory of Reciprocity," *Games and Economic Behavior* 54, no. 2 (February 2006): 293–315, https://doi.org/10.1016/j.geb.2005.03.001.

25. "The Important Role of Leaders in Advancing Human Sustainability," *Deloitte Insights*, June 11, 2025, https://www.deloitte.com/us/en/insights/topics/talent/workplace-well-being-research-2024.html.

26. "New survey: Company mission & culture matter more than compensation," *Glassdoor US*, accessed November 7, 2025, https://www.glassdoor.com/blog/mission-culture-survey.

27. Regina Dyerly, "The Myth of Replaceability: Preparing for the Loss of Key Employees," *Welcome to SHRM*, January 21, 2025, https://www.shrm.org/executive-network/insights/myth-replaceability-preparing-loss-key-employees.

28. "Science behind a Good Cultural Fit: Chapman & Co.," Default, accessed November 7, 2025, https://www.ccoleadership.com/resources/insight/the-science-behind-a-good-cultural-fit.

29. Justin Kruger and David Dunning, "Unskilled and Unaware of It: How Difficulties in Recognizing One's Own Incompetence Lead to Inflated Self-Assessments," *Journal of Personality and Social Psychology* 77, no. 6 (1999): 1121–34, https://doi.org/10.1037//0022-3514.77.6.1121.

30. Joel Schwartzberg, "How to Answer, 'Why Should We Hire You?' In an Interview," *Harvard Business Review*, November 8, 2024, https://hbr.org/2024/11/how-to-answer-why-should-we-hire-you-in-an-interview.

31. Joel Schwartzberg, "How to Answer 'Why Do You Want to Work Here?'" *Harvard Business Review*, August 3, 2022, https://hbr.org/2022/08/how-to-answer-why-do-you-want-to-work-here.

32. Marius Guenzel et al., "AI Personality Extraction from Faces: Labor Market Implications," *SSRN Electronic Journal*, 2025, https://doi.org/10.2139/ssrn.5089827.

33. Petri Hukkanen and Matti Keloharju, "Initial Offer Precision and M&A Outcomes," *Financial Management* 48, no. 1 (July 10, 2018): 291–310, https://doi.org/10.1111/fima.12229.

THANK YOU

First, I want to thank my family: my wife, Laura, and my three children, Zara, Eve, and Atlas. You've been my greatest source of purpose and strength. When I faced my own seasons of rejection. When I was told I was "too qualified," "too educated," or "too much" to be hired, you gave me the reason to keep going. Thank you for believing in me until I got that one "yes" that changed everything, and for standing beside me as I built a way to help others find theirs.

I also want to thank my parents. They showed me what resilience really looks like. No matter how many economic hardships they faced or how many doors were closed in their faces, they never stopped working, saving, and believing that something better was possible. They taught me that there's always something within your control — some small action, some piece of knowledge, some connection — that can turn your situation around. They gave me the mindset that one "yes," one idea, or one person can change your entire life. That belief built everything I've done since.

And finally, I want to thank the tens of thousands of incredible professionals I've had the privilege to work with over the past fifteen years. You are the reason this book exists. From former executives and inventors with dozens of patents, to scientists with hundreds of publications, to senior leaders in Fortune 100 and global organizations, to those who found themselves unexpectedly unemployed, driving for rideshare companies, serving coffee, or working overnight shifts, you've all shown me the true meaning of capability and courage.

Every one of you who allowed me to guide you through the process of repositioning yourself in the job market reminded me that this work isn't just about strategy, it's about rediscovering self-worth. You taught me that the hardest part of the job search isn't just convincing others of your value; it's remembering it yourself first. Thank you for opening your minds and hearts enough to believe that your story wasn't over. Helping you rediscover your confidence and your rightful place in the world of work has been my greatest professional honor.

ABOUT ISAIAH HANKEL

Isaiah Hankel is the Founder and CEO of Overqualified™, the leading career consultancy for experienced professionals who are ready to reclaim their value in today's job market. For more than 15 years, Isaiah has helped more than 20,000 highly capable professionals, most of them in their 40s, 50s, and 60s, with advanced degrees and decades of experience, land the roles they truly deserve at top organizations across every major sector.

Isaiah's industry-changing approach reframes what it means to be overqualified. His system teaches accomplished professionals how to communicate their worth, eliminate employer bias, and turn perceived obstacles into undeniable advantages. His articles, podcasts, and trainings reach millions of readers and listeners each year, empowering experienced job seekers to transition with confidence and purpose.

A three-time bestselling author, Isaiah's work has been featured in *Harvard Business Review*, *Nature*, *Forbes*, *The Guardian*, *Fast Company*, *Entrepreneur*, and *Success Magazine*. Through Overqualified™, he continues to lead a movement proving that deep experience isn't a liability; it's a competitive edge.

CONTACT

Website: Overqualified.com
Email: Isaiah@Overqualified.com
LinkedIn: LinkedIn.com/in/IsaiahHankel

www.ingramcontent.com/pod-product-compliance
Lightning Source LLC
LaVergne TN
LVHW052234110526
838202LV00095B/234